The

LESS-THAN-PERFECT RIDER

Overcoming Common Riding Problems

The

LESS-THAN-PERFECT RIDER

Overcoming Common Riding Problems

Lesley Bayley & Caroline Davis

HOWELL BOOK HOUSE

NEW YORK

First American Edition, 1994

Howell Book House
Macmillan USA
15 Columbus Circle
New York, NY 10023

Printed in Italy

Macmillan Publishing Company is part of the Maxwell Communication
Group of Companies.

Library of Congress Cataloging in Publication Data

Bayley, Lesley.
The less than perfect rider : overcoming common riding problems
Lesley Bayley and Caroline Davis : (photographs by Angus Murray).
1st American ed.
p.   cm.
Includes index.
ISBN 0–87605–976–0
1. Horsemanship.   I. Davis, Caroline.   II. Title.
SF309.B355   1994
798.2′3––dc20
93–33471
CIP

10 9 8 7 6 5 4 3 2

CONTENTS

INTRODUCTION

When watching top-class riders such as Mark Todd, John Whitaker, Bruce Davidson, Ginny Elliot (formerly Leng), Carol Lavell and Ferdi Eilberg, you may readily become convinced that 'being a good rider' is beyond your range of achievement. As they soar over huge fences with the greatest of ease or perform intricate dressage movements without appearing to do anything, the likelihood of your emulating them may seem extremely remote. Of course it would be wonderful to ride like these superstars: but, you tell yourself, they have the natural talent, the time, the opportunities, the horses . . . you can make their list of advantages seem endless – whereas your circumstances are, of course, much less favourable. And before you know it, you will have talked yourself into being a second-rate rider for the rest of your life! No doubt you will comfort yourself with numerous excuses:

■ 'I've got short legs so I'll never make a dressage rider – there's no hope of me ever achieving a deep seat';

■ 'I started to ride too late in life so riding in horse trials will have to remain a dream';

■ 'Of course, if I'd had the right horse then I'd have been more successful' . . .

But it's time to climb out of the comfort zone and prove yourself wrong! Perfect riders just do not exist: ask the successful top-class competitors, and they would soon tell you about their own faults – and you'd probably be surprised by how numerous those faults are! None of these riders think they are perfect, so why should *you* let yourself be put off by the fact that you have short legs, or are worried about jumping, or suffer from ring fright?

There's a saying that success is one per cent talent and 99 per cent perspiration. Our top riders only got where they are with years of hard work, and no doubt had plenty of bad times when things went wrong when they, too, questioned whether they were good enough, times when perhaps they felt like giving up. But the difference between these riders and those who never fulfil their potential is that whereas some people give up all too readily, others persist. Remember Aesop's fable about the hare and the tortoise? The race was won not by the faster creature but by the animal which, slowly but surely, kept on going.

Riding is very much like that: whether you are just learning, or trying to improve after years in the sport, it is such a demanding and challenging discipline that even after a lifetime's practice there is still more to learn.

Those who want to improve their riding must put it into perspective: there is no quick and easy way to success, and *every* rider, no matter how talented he appears, finds that his 'learning curve' levels out every now and then – for a frustrating period his riding seems to be making no progress at all, then suddenly the next piece clicks into position and he is off again. In this it is no different for the pupil struggling to master rising trot at a small equestrian centre, than it is for the one-horse owner aiming to make the riding club team or the professional rider whose goal may be the Hickstead Derby or Burghley Horse Trials. Of course everyone makes mistakes – for instance, Olympic eventer Ginny Elliot was eliminated from her first official horse trials because she missed out a fence. So resist the temptation to get too introspective when something does go wrong – just take a look at other riders, good and bad, and particularly the latter if your confidence is ebbing.

It is important to be a thinking, aware rider, constantly searching for a better understanding of your sport, your horse and yourself. However, do not concentrate on your shortcomings: think about how to make use of what you have, rather than bemoan what you lack. And achieving success in any sport, be it riding, golf, football or athletics, boils down to individual persistence, which ensures that every time you suffer a setback you pick yourself up, learn from the experience and move on; also to lots of determination; dedication; attention to detail; and a dash of talent!

In our sport we also have that vital element, *the horses*. Building a partnership with your mount is essential – for example, complete trust and confidence in his rider is vital for the event horse, particularly those who are asked extremely big questions when they tackle the likes of Badminton and Burghley cross-country courses. In fact mutual respect, understanding and communication comprise a vital foundation for any horse and rider combination. All too often riders expect horses to listen to them, but they neglect to listen to what the horse is saying: horses are great teachers and great levellers.

Finding a horse to suit you may not be easy, but if you take the view that you can learn something from each one, this will have a more positive effect than, for instance, thinking 'Oh no, not So & So, he's so difficult to sit to/get into canter/stop'.

No matter why you think you are a 'less-than-perfect rider', you *can* move towards becoming a better one. It will mean you may have to change your way of thinking about things – for instance, obstacles and problems need to be thought of as 'opportunities' – and it will involve commitment with a capital C. However, the rewards are great so take the plunge now!

Take a Look at Yourself

Less-than-perfect riders come in all shapes, sizes and ages, each with their own individual hang-ups and circumstances. Basically, what this book will show you is that:

1 You are not alone with your difficulties;
2 Positive thinking can work wonders;
3 Everyone can improve.

■ There is no short-term solution to riding success: a great deal of time and effort is needed, but it can be hugely rewarding

Before you can start to work on your imperfections you need to know what they are, and you are not always the best person to judge! Moreover some riders lack so much confidence that they can only see their faults, and fail to recognise their positive attributes. Others are just the opposite! If you have an instructor, then he or she can offer guidance regarding the areas you need to work on: for example, achieving an independent seat, or improving your rein contact.

But what do you do if there is no instructor available nearby? A knowledgeable friend can perhaps help, but he or she may not be able to recognise the true cause of your difficulties. Hence this book; you should be able to find the answers, and constructive help in the following chapters, also illustrations which cover many common problems and how they manifest themselves.

The following exercise may be useful: first make a list of the attributes that you think are vital for a good rider, then very carefully consider each of the points you have noted and mark the ones which you honestly feel apply to you. This is not the time to be modest, but equally you must be realistic or there will be no benefit in the exercise. If you feel that an attribute only partially applies to you – perhaps you feel your seat is reasonable but not 100 per cent independent – then write your comments alongside.

■ *Top right:* Riders of all levels have their own problems. It's much easier for someone on the ground to pick up on your difficulties and the reasons behind them

■ All riders suffer setbacks at times: sometimes it's in public eg a disappointment at a show; at other times it's a private affair eg you're schooling a horse at home and everything goes disastrously wrong. The secret to success is to analyse *what* went wrong and *why*, put it all into perspective and then set about correcting the problem/mistake

We asked several people to do this exercise, and below are the attributes they listed as necessary for a rider to qualify as 'good':

- Good position
- Excellent balance
- Sensitivity to the horse, and sympathetic understanding of its nature
- Truly independent seat
- Good co-ordination and being in complete control of the body
- Sensitive hands
- Being open-minded
- Positive thinking
- Riding which appears effortless
- Dedication
- Good reactions
- Long legs
- Confidence

When it came to matching the attributes of the ideal to themselves, our riders found no problem in marking the physical ones such as long legs, but felt obliged to qualify others as, for example, 'My hands are fine when I'm riding on the flat, but I tense when jumping and fix them into the horse's neck'; 'I'm fairly confident on my own horse, but not on anything strange'; 'My position is excellent – until the horse moves!' . . .

Take another look at your list: if you're unsure whether, for instance, your position is good or otherwise, study the information in chapter 1 but apply it to photographs or videos of yourself riding: study the photos or videos carefully, and you'll learn a lot about your current standard of riding. And do *not* be overwhelmed because there seem to be a great many areas you need to work on. None of our riders could truthfully say they had a truly independent seat or excellent balance, or many of the other pointers for a good rider, either! If everyone was *that* good there would be no need for this book!

The great news is that attributes such as balance and an independent seat can be worked on and achieved without too much difficulty. None of these miraculously happen: they take effort and time, factors which can be controlled by you.

What about factors which can't be affected by you, such as your body shape? In this respect, take a look at any equestrian sport and you'll see tall, short and medium-sized riders, old and young alike – to be successful you don't necessarily have to be tall, slim, elegant and perfectly proportioned. However, what you must do is learn how to make the most of yourself – for positive advice, see Chapter 3.

Perhaps you feel your mental attitude is holding you back. Advice on how to harness your mind power, and use it constructively, is given specifically in Chapter 3, and generally throughout this book. By utilising your mind to your advantage you'll be able to conquer any lack of confidence and anxiety crises, turn the likes of frustration and fear into motivational forces, and stop the fear of failure being such a limiting factor on your riding.

Having listed the aspects to be desired in a good rider, the same group of riders then detailed their fears about riding. These included the fear of:

- Falling off
- Not understanding what their instructor wants
- Being made to look a fool
- Causing injury to the horse through their own inadequacies
- Fear of what other people think
- Injury (and particularly the associated worry as to who would look after their families/horses, plus what an employer would think)
- Fear of not being as good as the rest of the group and of not riding as well as their instructor knows they can, thereby letting him down

No doubt you can identify with these fears, and can probably add your own: however, the point is that we *all* have fears and worries but it is how we deal with them that makes the difference between becoming a decent rider and staying as one of the crowd.

The Role Model

We all have riders we admire and long to emulate, so why not turn your respect for someone into a positive force? Study your chosen rider – what is it about him (or her) which makes him so special? Read any books or magazine articles by or about the subject: what do these tell you about the person, and how can any of this be applied to your circumstances? For instance, one of the co-authors of this book, Lesley, has been a great admirer of event rider Lucinda Green for many years; as a riding-school rider Lesley read Lucinda's books and quickly realised that this six-times Badminton winner had experienced all the ups and downs, frustrations,

doubts and self-recriminations that most other riders feel. So if you doubt your own ability at any time, comfort yourself with the thought that even world-class riders like Lucinda Green had to work hard to learn how to ride so well!

The Horse

The other vital ingredient in our equation is the importance of the horse. Equine stars such as Lucinda's Be Fair are few and far between, and most people will only ever ride 'ordinary' horses who are unlikely to compete at Badminton or the Horse of the Year show. But that is not to underestimate their value, and some of the most worthwhile lessons can be learnt from the most unlikely of horses: for example, Lucinda's Badminton winner Killaire was a horse many considered should never have left the hunting field, and one which was thought to lack the quality, speed and jumping ability needed in the successful event horse. But these people reckoned without Killaire's outstanding courage – he tried his heart out, and so notched up a place in equestrian history.

Thus keep your mind open, and be prepared to ride some less-than-perfect horses too! Your next mount might be a short-striding, cobby animal who leans on the forehand – but listen to him, think about how you can get the best from him, and you could learn a lot!

■ Jumping can be a source of great pleasure – or deep despair if you experience a confidence crisis. Cracking any deep-rooted anxieties or correcting any rider position problems will need expert help

1
UNDERSTANDING AND RIDING YOUR HORSE

If you watch horses moving at liberty in a field you will see how easily they accelerate, change pace, stop and turn. Loose-schooled over jumps they also operate with ease and grace, despite the fact that a horse carries 60 per cent of its weight on its forehand. However, with a rider on board the picture can change dramatically, for although Man has used horses for over five thousand years their physique is basically not designed to carry a rider. With training, horses can learn to shift the balance of their weight-carrying ability – for instance, the highly schooled dressage horse when it performs piaffe and passage. The majority of horses, though, are trained to such a level, and their riders are not as skilful as the top dressage competitors: thus every day these horses have to compensate for, or learn to cope with, their riders' lack of talent and balance. Moreover, the horse is usually expected to help his rider – yet so often a rider has very little idea of how his horse moves, or the effects that he, a person, will have upon his horse's way of going.

The Horse's Physique in Movement

The horse is a large, weighty, bulky creature whose body is pretty inflexible – yet many riders appear not to allow for this as they try to wrench him round a sharp turn! Negotiating a corner on a horse is rather like towing a boat: in the same way that the boat cannot bend itself around a corner, neither can the horse because its spine is not very flexible. A large cat such as a cheetah in motion can arch its back and really bring its hindlegs under its body. The horse, with his much more rigid structure, cannot do this as easily – in fact it is the stifle joint in the horse which allows him to move his hindlimbs as far fowards as he does when galloping.

But if horses cannot bend easily, how do gymkhana ponies apparently bend in and out of poles at high speed? The horse's thorax – that part of the body enclosed by the ribs – is suspended in the 'thoracic sling', a cradle of muscle between the horse's shoulder blades. As the ribcage moves so the horse's rigid thoracic spine has to move too, therefore allowing the animal's body to move. In fact the thorax can move laterally to a considerable degree. So, watch a pony going down a line of bending poles and you will see that the leg nearest each pole is tucked in and the opposite leg is pulled away, taking a longer, sweeping stride. As a result the body rolls within the thoracic sling.

When you consider the horse, you will appreciate that he carries weighty organs such as the intestines in the second half of his body, and that the whole of his weight is balanced on his hooves, relatively small weight-bearing areas. He is propelled along by his four limbs, and the task of getting him airborne lies largely with the hindlimbs, the hock joint being a hard-working element at all times. His head and neck are his 'balancing pole' freely movable and which he employs to help alter his centre of gravity.

Movement throughout the horse's body is impaired, if his saddle doesn't fit correctly. An ill-fitting saddle not only damages the area it lies upon, it also causes the horse to compensate its movement elsewhere to try and avoid discomfort.

The Horse's Paces

The walk: This is a four-time pace: each leg functions independently, and the spine moves up and down as well as from side to side. The feet are moved in this sequence: near-hind, near-fore, off-hind, off-fore, and a rider should be able to feel the hindlegs coming underneath. As a hindleg moves forwards, so the barrel of the horse's body sways to the opposite side; and each time a foreleg comes to the ground the horse nods his head. Therefore there is considerable movement, which a rider must allow for with his hands.

A rider needs a supple seat to allow for the movement of the horse's back muscles as the animal walks. The *latissimus dorsi* muscles lie under the saddle area, and if these are insufficiently or incorrectly developed then the horse will find it difficult to carry a rider; the way in which he moves will also be adversely affected.

If a rider is not supple and is merely a heavy weight on the horse's back, then the effect on the horse will be seen as a loss in suppleness, co-ordination and freedom of the gait.

To allow for the movement of the horse's back the rider needs to develop suppleness in his loin area – that is the body on each side of the spine between the hip bones and the false ribs. This can be achieved by learning how to move the seatbones alternately: for example, as the horse's right hindleg is lifted forwards the rider allows his right seatbone forwards. The movement should not be an exaggerated one – indeed, anyone watching would not know what was happening.

The trot: The horse moves his legs in diagonal pairs: off-fore and near-hind as one pair, near-fore and off-hind as the other pair. There is a moment of suspension as one diagonal pair is about to hit the ground and as the other pair has just left it. In trot the horse's shoulder blades swing back and forth, and his hips swing up and down as the hindlegs are bent and come under the body; this results in a rolling motion.

This is why initially riders find it difficult to sit to a horse's trot: learning to absorb the rolling motion via your own loins, spine and seat can take some time. Your upper body needs to be vertical; it can be helpful to think of sitting to the trot as if you are riding the crests of small waves.

With rising trot the rider's body is again vertical or very slightly inclined forwards, but the rising movement should be minimal. Instead of pulling or pushing the seat up, well out of the saddle (as is so often seen), think of the movement as being a forwards one, with the crotch just brushing the top of the saddle pommel.

There should never be daylight between the rider and the saddle when rising to the trot, and the seat should always be 'eased' into the rise and then the sit beat: to help you sit lightly, imagine that the saddle is made of fine bone china which will break if you thump down into it!

■*Top left:* The rider is slouching along with no rein contact, and this is reflected in the horse's walk

■*Left:* In trot the horse's legs move in diagonal pairs. Our model is demonstrating a lack of contact and leaning too far forward which not only looks untidy but is also ineffective

■ Although the rider has leaned forward and dropped her contact in this transition to canter, you can see clearly how the horse is pushing off from its near hind. The next combination of legs in the sequence will be the diagonal pair of the off hind and near fore, followed by the off fore

■ It is rarely necessary to gallop a horse, unless in training for advanced speed competition: but it is fun!

The canter: This has three beats with a moment of suspension; the sequence of legs when cantering on the right rein is as follows:

1 Near-hind;
2 Off-hind and near-fore together as a diagonal pair;
3 Off-fore;
4 Moment of suspension.

Again this pace has a rolling feel to it, brought about by the horse's hindquarters rising as the leading foreleg hits the ground and then falling during the moment of suspension when the horse lifts his head. A common fault is to try to absorb this rolling motion by swinging the upper body backwards and forwards: rather it should be the seat and loins which soak up the movement.

Maintaining a correct position at canter is difficult: a rider must be supple in the loins, and able to control the seat and upper body to avoid bouncing around in canter.

The gallop: A four-time pace, which is achieved as the diagonal pair on the canter sequence is broken; there are only ever two legs on the ground at any one time because of the increased speed of movement.

Rider Position

Over the years a riding position has evolved which is the most efficient and effective one. It allows the rider to influence the horse in the best possible way and at the same time look elegant.

Think of the rider's position as being three building blocks, placed on top of each other: the head and shoulders make up the first block, the body is the second, and the pelvis and legs are the third. Provided they are all in line and balanced there is no problem – but if one of the blocks is slightly out of line, then the whole structure becomes less stable. And if a block is seriously out of line, then the stack collapses.

It is therefore not surprising that so much emphasis is placed on the rider's seat, and his or her ability to ride in balance with the horse. That renowned school of horsemanship, the Spanish Riding School of Vienna, expects its young riding recruits to spend their first six months on the lunge – and they are already of a good standard when they join the school.

Before you even go near a horse, try the following exercise to help you understand the riding position: stand with your feet about twenty-four inches apart, with your body upright. Bend the knees slightly and glance down to check that you can just see your toes. Now look ahead again, and check that you are standing squarely on both feet. You should find that you can stay in this position, quite comfortably, for some time – and when you are sitting in the saddle it will be even easier to maintain this position.

Play about with this dismounted position – be sure you have adopted the correct one, with knees slightly bent, body upright, then change elements: for example, lean forwards slowly, and recognise at what point you come off balance. Shift your weight more onto one foot, and note the effect that that has. Be aware of how your balance and your body is affected – and remember that the horse will feel these changes too, and they will affect his balance. .

Seat and Balance

The rider should sit in the deepest part of the saddle, and this will place his weight over the horse's centre of gravity, so making it easier for the horse to carry the additional load. A horse which is unfortunate enough to be carrying a rider who is out of balance – sitting too far back in the saddle, or unable to sit still and bouncing all over the place – will manifest his discomfort in several ways: he may raise his head, hollow his back, swish his tail, try to dislodge his rider, be altogether reluctant to move. Further, a rider who, for instance, leans forwards to check if his horse is on the correct canter lead, can in fact unbalance his mount and make it stumble.

A good saddle should place you in its deepest part; if it is not big enough for you, then you will be at a disadvantage as you will not be sitting in the deepest, central part.

You sit on the triangle of your two seatbones and your pelvic fork. An easy exercise on horseback to locate the seatbones is to slip the feet out of the stirrups and bring the knees up as high as you can, without leaning backwards too much: you should now be able to

■ Locating your seat bones

feel the two bones. (Make sure someone holds your horse while you execute this exercise.) Then re-take your stirrups – your instructor will check your position from behind to see if there is any unlevelness.

Think also of pressing the hip joints forwards slightly – this will keep the pelvis upright. You can double-check by looking at the side of your jodhpurs – the seams should be upright and at right-angles to the horse's back. Remember that the rider's hips and shoulders should stay square with the horse as it moves.

From the side it should be possible to draw an imaginary line straight through the rider's ear, shoulder, hip and heel.

If you are checking a friend's position, look from behind and notice the central seam of his or her jodhpurs: it should align with the central seam of the saddle cantle. If it doesn't it is probably because he/she has collapsed a hip on one side.

Your horse cannot be expected to move straight if you are not sitting straight! From behind it should be possible to run a line down the centre of your body to produce two equal halves.

The Upper Body

The upper body needs to be tall but relaxed: tension is the enemy of riders! Your aim should be to maintain your riding position with the minimum of effort and tension, so that you can stay in balance with your horse thus enabling him to do his job with the minimum of effort. Any loss of position or balance on your part will be immediately reflected in the way your horse goes, so learn to listen to what the horse is telling you. If you suddenly find that the horse is moving to the left instead of going straight, check that *you* have not altered your weight distribution and thereby suggested that he do so! Similarly, any sudden behavioural changes must have a reason – around a turn you may have altered your hand position so that your schooling whip is touching your horse's flank. He may react by kicking out.

Remember that your head is a heavy part of your body, so try to avoid tilting it or looking down: from the rear it should be square on your shoulders.

Think of keeping your shoulders over your hips, and of their being level; try not to let them droop forwards. Think of expanding your chest and lifting your diaphragm: put a couple of fingers under the bottom of your ribcage in the centre, and imagine that you can hook your fingers under the ribs; as you breathe in gently, imagine that you are lifting your ribcage forwards and up. Let your shoulders drop backwards too,

so that the blades are closer together. Bring this image and feeling into action every time you feel your upper body slumping.

The Arms and Hands

Your arms should be relaxed along your sides with the elbows tucked in so that the inside of your sleeve brushes gently against your jacket. Ideally there ought to be a straight line along the lower arm, through the wrist, hand and along the rein to the horse's mouth. This line will be broken if the horse throws his head up as the rider would not raise the hands too. It may also be broken in particular circumstances – for example, a

An effective, tidy and correct riding position. The rider is:

alert and aware of what's happening around her, therefore ready to give directions to the horse as needed;

maintaining a relaxed, yet constant, contact with the horse's mouth;

sitting on her seatbones in the deepest part of the saddle;

keeping the inside of her thighs against the saddle and her lower legs against the horse's sides, both for security and aid effectiveness. Although the legs are 'on', they are relaxed; knees and ankles are 'soft', with the knees and the toes pointing forwards; the stirrup irons are positioned on the balls of the feet, although the feet could be 'pushed home' a little more

rider may occasionally lower the hands when school-ing a horse.

A rider's hands should be held level and as a pair, and as regards rein contact, imagine you are holding a live bird – tightly enough to prevent him flying off, but not so tight that you injure him. Avoid clenching the hands or you will create tension and this will result in your fixing them. Keep the thumbs uppermost and hold the hands about three inches above the saddle. Do not let them rest on the horse's neck, and try to avoid turning the wrists in or out.

Think of your hands as belonging to the horse: they guide and control him, but should never restrict or hurt him.

The Legs and Feet

The rider's legs should hang in a relaxed way – if the saddle is fitted correctly and the leg is in the correct position, the stirrup leather will hang straight down. The legs should be relaxed down the horse's sides, the thigh flat against the saddle and the lower leg touching the horse's side. The knee should point to the front, but should not be clamped in against the saddle – imagine a fist placed between your knee and the saddle. Where exactly the rider's lower leg touches the horse's side will depend on the length of the rider's leg (and assum-ing that the rider is matched to the horse in terms of size).

Let your feet rest in the stirrups with just enough weight to keep the stirrups in place (remembering that the stirrup should be on the ball of the foot). Think of your heel being lower than your toe – but don't force the ankle down, or you will create stiffness throughout the leg. The toes should point forwards, though if both or one of your feet has a natural tendency to stick out, you will just have to make the best of it! Trying to force yourself into a totally unnatural position will only result in tension everywhere.

The joints of your legs act as shock absorbers to help maintain balance and agility. Remember that still legs produce more effective aids – if your legs move too much, the horse will learn to ignore them.

This describes the ideal riding position, but let us quickly reassure all those who feel that they fall far short because of their short legs or their tubby bodies! Advice on how to make the most of your body shape can be found in Chapter 3; but remember that whatever your body looks like, there are other factors which you *can* influence. For instance, suppleness; the ability to use your weight effectively; the development of 'feel' for the horse's movement; and an understanding of how the horse is put together, and how this affects the way he moves.

Set yourself the goals of achieving a secure, independent seat and of applying the aids as correctly and discreetly as possible. You might also undertake to approach your riding with an open mind; to be a consistent, quiet rider; to use your brain, and think about what you are doing and why; and to have patience – if you can achieve all this, then you will already be on the way to becoming a more sensitive and better rider.

Communicating with the Horse

Every time you ride, a subtle and civilised conversation should take place between you and the horse. By means of the natural aids (your seat and weight, your legs, hands, voice and thought) you will be asking the horse to move, to change direction and pace, to work in a particular shape (outline), to stop, and to negotiate obstacles or hazards such as roadworks. Ideally the horse should respond positively as soon as you give him your request. If he doesn't, there could be a number of reasons why:

● He doesn't understand what is wanted of him
● He is not in a position to obey
● He has not reached the stage of training or of muscular development or suppleness needed in order to respond to your request
● He is in pain or is uncomfortable

The rider should be *riding* the horse, and should not be merely a passenger; thus to produce a good performance from the horse, he must use the aids effectively when he asks for what he wants. If he uses certain aids and the horse does not respond, then he must ask himself *why* the lines of communication between himself and the horse have broken down. This could be for any one or a combination of the following reasons:

● Rider sends confusing or conflicting messages to the horse: for example, the legs say 'go', but the hands are saying 'stop', and very roughly because the rider is using the reins to balance himself.
● Rider is maintaining only an intermittent conversation with the horse – for example, he keeps taking his legs off the horse's flanks.
● Poor preparation of the horse by the rider: asking a horse for a canter transition from an idle walk.
● Rider being unclear about the aids required for a specific movement; thus only half a message is sent to the horse, who is then expected to understand and add the other half of the message himself!

Let us consider the various natural aids and how they affect the horse.

The Rider's Seat and Weight

A rider can only use the seat aids beneficially if he sits correctly, softly and quietly with his weight equally distributed on both seatbones. It is therefore a priority to develop an independent seat or you will never be able to allow your horse to remain supple and swing through his back. Once you can feel the horse's hindlegs coming underneath him, and your seat is independent enough to allow you to use it without affecting other parts of your body, then your seat aids can be used as follows:

● To lighten or ease your weight on your seatbones and allow the horse's back to come up
● To allow the horse's back muscles to swing by sitting passively with supple loins and hips

● To ask for rhythm
● To engage the hindquarters and bring the hindlegs further underneath (when used in conjunction with the back and legs)

Through your seat you have a major influence on the horse's impulsion, outline and direction – but you cannot hope to feel what is happening to the horse underneath you unless you know what is happening with your own seat, and you can't see this yourself. It is therefore important to ask an instructor or friend to check your position regularly so you avoid slipping into any bad habits.

Remember that on straight lines your seat should be central, whereas for turns, circles, in canter and for lateral work your weight will be slightly to the inside to help your horse move in a balanced way.

■ Here the rider is turning her knee out too far, resulting in a twisted ankle, and so the ball of the foot is not level on the stirrup iron.

Position faults are easy for onlookers to pick out, but riders themselves often don't realise when something is wrong. However, there are ways of telling when things are not quite right:

■ Your horse doesn't perform as well as usual, ie he ignores your aids; feels 'stiff'; misbehaves; doesn't feel 'right'.
■ You experience pain or a feeling of 'tightness' that you don't normally suffer from.
■ You feel lop-sided or awkward.

Whenever you ride, whether schooling or simply hacking out, remember to give yourself a position check every so often. Mental self-instructions such as 'head-up, lift the diaphragm, sit on seatbones, heels down, relax' make a world of difference to how you feel and how your horse goes.

The Rider's Legs

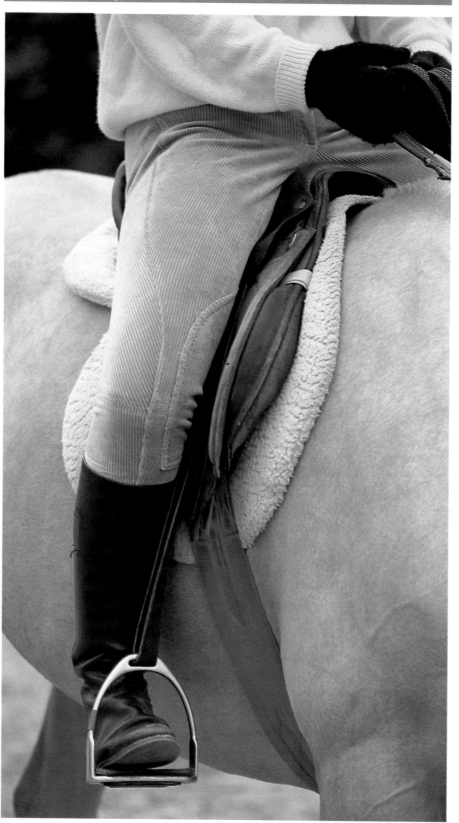

■ *Opposite:* The rider's legs can be used on the girth (*above*), or behind the girth (*below*) to control the horse's quarters as required.

■ *Left:* It is the rider's lower leg which is 'talking' to the horse, but his thigh also plays an important part: together with the weight of the upper body, the thighs help the effectiveness of the seat. The inside of the thigh needs to be as flat as possible against the saddle, as this allows the lower leg to be placed in much closer contact to the horse (*above*). You are also then able to use your lower leg without interfering with your seat.

■ It is the rider's lower leg which is 'talking' to the horse, but his thigh also plays an important part: together with the weight of the upper body, the thighs help the effectiveness of the seat. The inside of the thigh needs to be as flat as possible against the saddle, as this allows the lower leg to be placed in much closer contact to the horse. You are also then able to use your lower leg without interfering with your seat.

The legs are used to create forward movement; to activate the horse's hindquarters; to indicate direction and control the position of the horse; and to move the horse laterally (sideways). They may be used together or separately, but the inside of the lower leg should always remain in contact with the horse's flanks. In this way the rider is keeping a conversation going – that is, his legs are saying 'I'm here' all the time, and then by subtle squeezes or nudges, he can ask for more from the horse.

For instance, by closing both legs on the horse's sides he asks the horse to move forwards; in this he takes advantage of the horse's natural instinct to move away or 'escape' from pressure. And by using one leg more specifically than the other and in conjunction with the seat and hand, a rider may ask a horse to move sideways and forwards. When a leg aid is used, the rider's knee and thigh should remain relaxed on the saddle while the lower leg applies the aid.

On circles, the rider's leg aids have distinct uses. The inside leg – the rider's leg closest to the centre of the circle or on the inside of the bend – asks for more impulsion by encouraging the horse to move the hindleg more energetically forwards on that side; he thus brings the leg further underneath himself, but without covering the ground more quickly. To achieve this the rider has to time the aid very carefully so that the aid is felt as the horse's inside hindleg comes off the ground; then the horse can respond to the aid and bring his leg further underneath him. However, the rider needs to contain the increased energy in his hands and seat so that the horse does not simply speed up.

The inside leg is also used on circles in conjunction with the reins to achieve a correct bend to the inside. In this case the rider's leg aid is likely to be more of a soft squeeze than the distinct nudge which asks for increased impulsion.

In the same way as a horse will evade pressure on the ribs from the rider's inside leg by bringing his leg forwards and under his body, so he will also turn the quarters slightly away from the rider's inside leg aid. If the rider does not correct this deviation by placing his outside leg (the leg furthest away from the centre of the circle) slightly behind the girth, then the horse will travel somewhat sideways instead of the hind hoofprints following in the tracks of the front feet, which is what we want when moving on a circle.

When bringing his outside leg back in order to control the horse's quarters, a rider must guard against taking the leg so far back that he tips himself off balance or upsets his co-ordination.

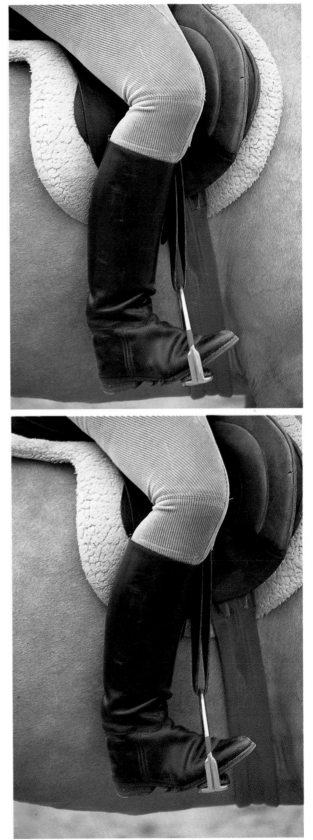

The Rider's Hands

All the aids are used in conjunction with each other, with the legs and seat being used before the hands. The rider's hands contain the impulsion created by his seat and legs; they control the speed; help the horse balance himself; indicate direction; control the bend; and help to maintain outline.

Think of the hands as being the telephone lines, via the reins and bit, to the horse's brain; and remember that the hands are irrefutably linked to the wrists, arms and shoulders: all four parts need to be supple and to work together well in order to maintain a constant sympathetic contact with the horse's mouth.

■ When negotiating a corner, turn your thumb-nail (not the whole hand) to point towards where you want to go. This often helps a rider to make better turns without altering the amount of contact or pulling back on the reins.

■ The inside hand 'takes' to indicate flexion/direction while the outside hand 'gives' to allow flexion and enable the horse to turn.

It is vital that:

■ The hands never pull backwards. You must be sensitive in the use of your hands in order to give the horse confidence – otherwise you may convince him that his discomfort and pain are inevitable when you ride!
■ A rider's hands need to remain still in relation to the movement of the horse – and of course, should be independent of other parts of the rider's body.

■ A consistent rein contact is essential for the horse or he will lose his sense of security and his confidence will be undermined. This contact should be light and sympathetic, with the same weight of contact being kept throughout all gaits; just because the horse is going faster there is no need to adopt a much stronger contact.

You can use your hand aids in a number of ways:

■ By momentarily ceasing to follow or to allow for the horse's movement with your hands, arms and shoulders, you are asking him to slow down or halt (providing that at the same time your leg and seat aids are also employed).
■ The fingers can be squeezed around the rein, as, for example, when asking for a half-halt.
■ When working on a circle, the inside hand asks or shows the

direction wanted from the horse whilst the outside hand regulates the speed and pace and helps balance the horse by controlling the bend through his neck around the circle. If, for instance, the horse is looking too much to the inside, then the rider needs to increase the weight felt on the outside rein and allow with the inside rein so that the horse's head and neck moves into the right position – that is, it follows the curve of the circle. Once this has been regained, then equal weight can be re-established.

■ The rider's voice is an aid which is often forgotten, but the rider's voice can be used most effectively to encourage, soothe, correct or reward a horse. It is the *tone* of voice used to which the horse will react – although with training he will learn to recognise certain words.

Positive Thinking

Think things out: careful forethought can be a powerful influence. Prepare well in advance for what you plan to do, as you will then find that the execution of, say, a particular movement will be easier. Pretend you are a rider you admire, as this will take the focus of your attention off your own shortcomings and the end result will undoubtedly be an improved performance from you!

Adaptability is a useful quality in a rider; horses and humans being individuals, it is quite likely that things may not happen as they are supposed to in books! So use your brain and flexibility to adapt yourself and to work out how you might apply the basic principles of riding to your particular situation.

Choosing the Right Instructor

It cannot be stressed enough how important it is to be able to communicate with your instructor. A teacher who makes your lessons fun, and who improves your technique and feeling of self-esteem is worth his/her weight in gold! Equally you must respond to your teacher, since for an instructor there is nothing worse than trying to help a pupil who will not speak or say how she/he feels, or has a permanently blank expression on his/her face. Instructors can only really help if pupils help themselves to become better, sympathetic and thinking riders.

It is also vital that you feel you can trust your instructor implicitly, and know that he/she will not put either you or your horse at risk by asking you to do something that is beyond your capability. He/she should inspire you with confidence and faith in your own abilities, but not give you false hope.

He/she should be friendly and helpful, yet retain professionalism in his/her appearance and manner, and be strict *up to a point* – there is a definite line between a teacher being too soft and too firm. He/she should have the ability to relate to, and teach people to ride *as individuals* and not always 'by the book'; it is essential that an instructor can deviate from basic techniques to help improve his/her pupils, as what works for one may not work for another.

If you don't respect and like your instructor, then you are not likely to get the best from your riding.

■ Finding an instructor who makes learning fun, as well as interesting, can be difficult – but it's worth it. Make sure that your instructor gets on with your horse, as well as with you

■ Good riding schools start their clients off on the lunge or lead rein to develop their balance and co-ordination.
■ Novice riders will not progress if their mounts, initially, are stubborn, stiff or disobedient.
■ When your riding skills have developed, it is beneficial to ride different animals of varying temperaments and abilities.
■ Expect 'lows' as well as 'highs' when you are learning to ride. Don't let the low points depress you, persevere and everything will come right eventually.

Finding an Instructor

The best way is by word of mouth, so ask riding friends if they can recommend anyone. Failing that, enquire at local livery yards and riding schools; and if at all possible, try to see your proposed instructor in action teaching others – that way you will soon get a good idea of whether she/he will suit you.

Find out what level of instruction he/she offers – this is essential if you want to progress higher up the ladder in your chosen equestrian sphere. Many instructors specialise in certain areas or disciplines – for example, dressage, combined training, show jumping, exam preparation, nervous riders or children – so do enquire as to whether your proposed instructor has any special interest.

Be honest about what you want from tuition. A good instructor takes pride in his/her work and expects a pupil to be honest, and to have the desire to ride well to his/her chosen level. Therefore tell your instructor exactly what you require from lessons, and indicate the standard you wish to achieve.

Finding an instructor who suits both you and your horse is often very much a case of trial and error. Thus if you are not satisfied with your progress, and cannot make headway by explaining how you feel to your teacher, then it is time for you to move on and look elsewhere.

NOTE: Do ensure that your instructor has adequate insurance cover.

The Riding School

Choosing a riding school when you are learning to ride isn't always easy, and first of all you must know how to differentiate between good and bad ones.

A good school should be clean and relatively tidy. It should be licensed, and have adequate insurance to protect clients in case of non-accidental injury. The horses should look healthy, and should be kind, steady (yet forward-going), well mannered and well schooled.

Tack should be modern and in good, supple condition – although don't expect it to be always beautifully clean. However, you should always expect your horse to be provided with a neckstrap, for you to hang on to if necessary.

Your horse should match your size and weight, although it is preferable for complete novices or nervous riders to be mounted on a smaller horse, albeit well up to their weight. A beginner will not then be put off riding at first sight of his mount!

Summary

Points to note:

■ The aids are not used in isolation – leg, seat and hand aids are applied at the same time though the relative strength of each aid may differ.

■ As your riding progresses so you will understand that the aids have many subtleties and refinements.

■ Do not practise sitting trot on young horses as their back muscles are often not sufficiently strong to cope with unbalanced, bouncing riders – or even well balanced riders.

■ Do not try to achieve a deep seat by lengthening your stirrups too much too soon.

■ If your horse is very wide and round it will be difficult for you to adopt a good leg position since your hip-joint movement will be restricted.

■ Stiffness in your back, neck or shoulders will affect the sensitivity of your hand aids.

Points to put into action:

■ Carry out some warming-up and loosening-up exercises out of the saddle before you mount and school your horse.

■ Spend some time each day working without stirrups – though no more than 10 minutes – in order to develop your seat. However, bouncing about uncontrollably will not help either you or your horse, so take hold of the pommel with your inside hand to steady yourself if necessary.

■ Imagine you are stretching your pelvis over the saddle – this will help you achieve a closer seat.

■ To really improve your riding, book yourself some lunge lessons. It is more beneficial to have four short sessions on consecutive days than one long session every week.

■ As you ride, mentally run through a checklist of your position. Here our model is concentrating too hard, and is looking down

The Aids in Action

Moving off:
1 Check your position
2 Maintain a light, elastic rein contact
3 Apply extra pressure with both legs by the girth – a series of quick vibrant touches, not a steady squeeze.

Upward transitions within a pace:
(eg from working trot to medium trot):
1 Check position
2 Half-halt to increase engagement of hindlegs
3 Apply legs by girth to lengthen horse's stride
4 Contain impulsion via the reins, but allow horse to lengthen his outline, whilst maintaining a supple seat so that the horse can swing his back.

Downward transitions:
1 Check position
2 Use half-halts on outside rein
3 Use seat and legs to engage hindquarters and lighten forehand
4 Restrain with reins, but do not restrict (slowing down instruction usually given with outside rein)
5 As soon as new gait is achieved, ride forwards using seat and legs to ensure that rhythm of new gait is quickly established.

To turn or circle:
1 Check position
2 Squeeze fingers on inside rein intermittently to establish a more flexible contact and indicate a slight bend
3 Turn body to inside, putting slightly more weight into inside stirrup
4 Use outside rein to allow for bend of horse's head and neck but maintaining a constant contact. May need to apply a half-halt to control the pace
5 Use both legs and supple seat to maintain impulsion. Inside leg on the girth is the dominant aid, asking the horse to bring his hindleg further underneath on that side so he can follow the true line of the circle. The outside leg is ready to act

if the horse's hindquarters swing out.
NOTE: Remember to ride inside leg to outside rein so the horse is bent around your inside leg with his hindlegs following in the track of the front legs.

Ways in which communication is disrupted:
■ The rider keeps his legs off the horse for most of the time, only suddenly clamping them on when he wants to go faster. This is not fair to the horse, since for most of the time the rider does not 'talk' to him, but then he suddenly demands action.
■ Insufficient rein contact – a common fault which a rider must make a determined effort to conquer. Often the rein contact is lost on one rein only (usually the outside rein) when riding circles or turns. Regular lessons are worthwhile because a good instructor should pick up faults like this and make you aware of them, and help you to correct them.
■ Constant nagging from a rider's legs or hands tends to result in the horse ignoring signals.
■ Horses which are very forward-going often worry some riders, who will abandon all leg contact in the belief that this will prevent the horse 'running off' with them. However, in doing this a rider is effectively removing a large chunk of his 'control mechanism' over a horse; nor is it helping the horse, especially if this style of riding is practised over a long period – the horse will soon lose that sense of security of a rider communicating with him; further, he may react badly or become worried when someone does try to ride him properly, with their legs in constant contact.

2
SAFETY AND COMFORT

There is no doubt about it, riding is a risk sport but, as with anything, the risk is intensified if you fail to take sensible precautions when you ride and are around horses. Thousands of riders receive hospital treatment for horse-related accidents every year, but a large proportion of these accidents could have been prevented had the unfortunate victims taken reasonable precautions.

If you are to be as safe and comfortable in the saddle as possible, correct and comfortable clothing and equipment are all-important, as is attention to rider fitness, capabilities and know-how. All in all, there's a bit more to responsible riding than simply buying a pair of jodhpurs and climbing aboard any old horse!

To help you make your hobby as pain-free and pleasant as possible, this chapter provides invaluable information on what to wear, choosing the most suitable equipment, how to find a good safe riding school, coping with allergies and physical ailments, as well as how you can avoid injury.

Clothing

What you wear when you ride is a matter of personal choice, but for safety's sake it is essential to recognise the basic necessities of head protection and appropriate footwear. And then the old adage of looking good to feel good certainly applies to riders: nothing boosts confidence more than knowing you look smart, so select riding gear that not only feels comfortable and makes riding as easy as possible, but suits you too. Quite apart from your own likes or dislikes, there are other factors to be considered when shopping – your shape, height, size, and any disabilities you might have; all will determine what clothing you wear.

Hats/Helmets

A riding hat is probably the first item of riding gear that many people buy, simply because it is the most important. The more you wear it, the sooner it will become moulded to your head shape and feel at its most comfortable. It can be confusing when you first buy one because of all the makes, weights and designs on the market. However, be sure that you buy one which conforms to current safety standards (in the UK this is BS 4472 and/or BS 6473 and in the US ASTM/SE1); a good retailer should be able to fit your hat correctly, and ensure that you know how to fasten the harness properly and safely. Shop around and try on as many makes and designs as possible to find the one that you feel most at home in.

Safety harnesses vary, too. Some hats have a basic harness that just fastens under the chin, but these have the distinct disadvantage in that if you fall, it is all too easy for the hat to slip back and for the harness to throttle you. Pick a hat with a snugly fitting chin-cup, preferably made of leather or soft moulded plastic. Some companies will make hats to measure if you cannot find a ready-made one.

If you choose a skull cap, try on as many different covers as you can to find one that fits your hat well, and is flattering. If you don't choose carefully and are unhappy with the result, it will not enhance your confidence when you ride as you will be fretting about your appearance.

■ When you choose a riding hat, make sure that it is comfortable, well-fitting and conforms to recognised, up-to-date safety requirements. Too tight and your hat will cause headaches; too loose and it will not provide maximum protection in the event of a fall

At the moment a new, improved European hat standard is being considered. This is likely to replace the current BS standards as previously stated.

To offer better protection than at present, a new standard will invariably mean larger hats – to accommodate extra shock-absorbing materials.

Although this style may look somewhat ugly, especially to traditionalists, riders must get their priorities right – better to look less than elegant, than lose your life or suffer brain damage. In any case, you'll soon get used to these hats if you have to wear them – remember when compulsory seat-belt wearing came into being?!

■ Pick boots to suit your budget, but more importantly to suit your requirements. Although fairly expensive, leather boots will last for years if they are cared for properly

■ **Note:** Once a hat has received a direct blow it should be discarded and a new one bought, because even if you can discern no visible damage, its impact-absorbing qualities will have been substantially reduced.

Boots

Boots, like hats, become an intensely personal item to many riders. Once 'worn in' and moulded to a certain shape, they become an extension of the wearer and help him/her to attain and keep the correct and strongest leg position possible. To this end, it is important to find the sort of boot that suits you best.

Whether you wear long or short boots for casual riding is purely a matter of choice. Long boots give more support than short ones, but only if they fit the legs and feet properly. Loose boots will flap, whilst too-tight boots will restrict movement and can cause cramp.

Long leather boots Essentially boots are worn to protect the legs, for example, from branches and against careless manoeuvring of gate-posts when out hacking; to provide support to the ankle joint; and to help protect the toes and feet if your horse stands on you. The low heel is designed to prevent the foot slipping right through the stirrup iron.

Long leather riding boots are undoubtedly the best

answer, and if they are made to measure they are bound to fit you well. Their only disadvantage is that they are expensive, especially tailored ones. However, cared for properly – and it is worth investing in a pair of well-fitting trees to prevent the boots wrinkling – a good pair of boots may last ten years.

Synthetic boots　Second-best to long leather boots are the synthetic sort, the top end of the price range being better than the cheap, hard rubber varieties. These mould to the legs and feet, and some makes are manufactured in up to a hundred length and width fittings; so even those people with the shortest and thickest calves should be able to find ones to fit.

Some makes have a leather foot with a synthetic upper, thus providing the support of long leather boots but with the advantage of being far cheaper.

Jodhpur boots　Jodhpur boots provide a fair amount of ankle joint support and are a boon to those who simply cannot find long boots to fit. They are also cooler in summer, though to ward off wet or wintry weather you will need to wear chaps or gaiters.

Synthetic jodhpur boots are also available; these are ideal for smart wear around the yard, without the risk of mud and wet ruining them.

Gaiters

Gaiters, either of suede or finished leather, are ideal for people with thick or thin calves who find it difficult to find long boots that fit properly. Gaiters are worn over jodhpur boots and either jeans or jodhpurs.

Shirts

For casual tidiness many riders prefer to wear a polo shirt, which looks smart either alone or worn under a sweater. However, for those with less-than-perfect necks, either too thin or too thick, nothing can be more flattering than a stock shirt, where a stock collar is incorporated into the shirt neck.

The stock collar, or a conventional stock, is a great help to those riders who have a tendency to look down – the collar helps prevent this and reminds people when their chins are dipping. A conventional stock can also benefit those riders who suffer from neck pain, as it provides support when fitted properly.

As regards sweaters to be worn over shirts, for casual wear the classic Guernsey sweater is particularly flattering to riders of both sexes and of all shapes and sizes.

■ For smart, practical and easy wear, you can't beat a stock-collared shirt!

Breeches and Jodhpurs

Few of us possess a perfect figure, and many find that jodhs and breeches tend to highlight those areas we would rather not show! It pays therefore to choose your leg-wear with extreme care, and if possible when buying jodhs take along a truthful friend to help you make the right decision.

Whatever design you choose, be sure to select a cloth of good quality and weight as this will not betray any underwear lines. Choose a colour that is both flattering and practical for casual riding.

For showing, it is even more important to choose a good grade cloth for beige, cream or white jodhs if unsightly curves and underwear lines are not to be seen.

Many manufacturers now cater for those with a disability, and will make to measure at little extra cost.

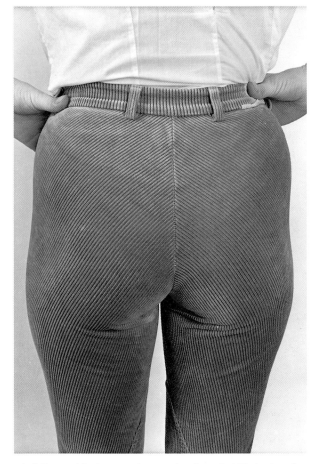

Men When wearing breeches, men should also wear good supportive underwear. Do not buy breeches which look and feel as though they've been painted on or you will not be comfortable – mentally as well as physically – and this will hinder your ease when on board your horse. Again, choose a heavy-ish nylon or cotton mix twill as jodhs and breeches look smarter and feel less uncomfortable.

Women Those who are tall and slim will have little problem in finding jodhs that look good; but take note that baggy jodhs will look dreadful, and if too loose they will rub and cause soreness.

Modern tailored jodhs and breeches with wide thighs (similar to the old cavalry style) usually look great on all sizes, even pear-shaped women, and are certainly extremely comfortable. However, those on the large side and without much of a waist should avoid these as they will accentuate the body shape rather than flatter it. In this case, stick to conventionally shaped jodhs in a fairly heavy material.

The best jodhpur/breeches materials for the less-than-perfect shape are cord; heavy nylon/nylon twill; and a good weight cotton/lycra.

Leather-seated jodhpurs or breeches provide a better grip in the saddle and thus afford a more secure seat. However, this can work the other way, of course, and make seat movement tricky.

Underwear

Problems are more likely to be encountered by those who are over-large: men can make life in the saddle more comfortable with the aid of a jockstrap and/or padded 'longjohns', but women have a tougher time if they possess a fuller figure. Support briefs will hold curves in and streamline the bottom half, but the main problem comes up top! It is essential to wear a supportive sports bra or top to alleviate discomfort. There are equestrian sports tops on the market, but the 38in cup and over needs a little more support than these tops provide.

Large women may benefit from wearing a good sports bra with the additional support of a sports support top worn over it.

Joint Supports

Stiff or sore elbow, wrist, knee and ankle joints can be helped with a sports support. Your doctor should be able to advise you on the best type to wear.

■ *Left:* Be careful when you buy breeches or jodhpurs, otherwise you can end up looking like this! On a hip-and-thigh-heavy figure like this, lightweight material simply won't hold your curves in check – it will cruelly highlight them! Choose a heavier material instead, preferably with lycra support
■ *Above:* That's better! The same rider as in the previous photograph looks a whole lot better when wearing well-fitting breeches in a heavier weight and elasticated cloth

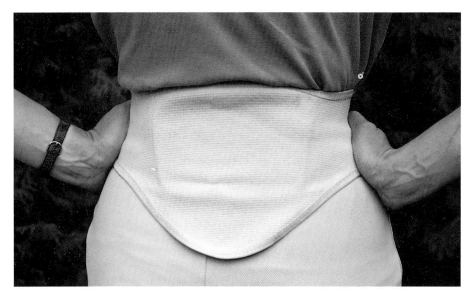

■ If you suffer from aches and pains in your back area when riding, a correctly fitted back support can provide immense relief, as well as promote good posture

Back Supports

Many riders suffer from a 'bad back': this is largely due to the undue stress that riding imposes on the back, also to carrying heavy loads around the yard. Aches and pains in and out of the saddle can be substantially eased by wearing a good back support: this helps to prevent jarring, and holds the joints in place a little more effectively when the back is under strain.

Back and shoulder supports are of immense help to riders who tend to slouch because they act both as a reminder and as a 'brace', encouraging the wearer to sit tall.

Sight Aids

Riders who need sight aids must wear either spectacles or contact lenses, and there are advantages and disadvantages to both.

Contact lenses: There are different types of contact lenses available, and what suits one individual may not suit another, both as regards comfort and ease of vision. The two main lens types are hard or soft, and you should choose whichever you feel most comfortable in. The only disadvantage of wearing lenses is that when dust or straw gets into your eyes it will cause irritation; but this is far outweighed by the fact that lenses avoid all those problems of misting up and rain-obscured vision which trouble spectacle wearers – not to mention the feeling of pure freedom they afford!

From the safety aspect (in the UK only), ensure that your Duvaxyn rider information card states that you wear contact lenses and carry the card at all times when you ride – in a pocket, not in your hat!

If you cannot cope with contact lenses, you can still make life more comfortable and safe by choosing spectacles carefully.

Spectacles: It cannot be denied that glasses can be a thorough nuisance when riding, and might also add to injury in the event of a fall: riders have been known to have escaped unscathed from a fall, apart from a broken or badly bruised nose where the hat has borne down on the bridge of the glasses.

Other disadvantages of wearing specs are that they mist up and slide down wet noses, and you can't always see where you are going in rain!

Riders should ensure that their spectacles have plastic safety lenses, not glass ones; ordinary glass lenses will shatter into tiny, lethal splinters under a blow, whereas plastic lenses will not. It pays to consult your optician to find the best option for you as regards plastic safety lenses and light frames.

Spectacle technology has come a long way – for example, if your eyesight is particularly bad you no longer have to put up with dense, weighty frames to support thick lenses. Specially formulated coatings and materials mean that the width and weight of lenses can now be dramatically reduced, even for the most short-sighted, so they can be contained in lighter frames. For riding it may be best to choose specs with wrap-around side-pieces, as these will stay in place better.

Whichever your option, be sure that you pick a hat with a harness that feels comfortable, and in particular one that doesn't put pressure on spectacle side-pieces.

Tack

The type of tack that is used on the horse has great bearing on a rider's position and comfort. For example, a saddle must fit and flatter the shape, rather than highlight imperfections and thus be lacking in security and comfort. Some people, both able and disabled, prefer to ride in Western tack, finding it more comfortable and secure.

For those that have difficulty in keeping their seat and leg positions, a deep and/or suede-seated saddle usually provides extra stability. The positioning of the knee and/or thigh rolls, plus the height of pommel and cantle, will also determine how comfortable a rider finds a saddle.

Take into account the length of the saddle flaps, as nothing is more frustrating than continually catching your boot tops on the bottom of the flaps. Besides, if the flaps are too long it may be difficult to put the legs on the horse's sides to any effect. Therefore pick a saddle that corresponds to your height, shape and weight.

Some people prefer synthetic saddles: they are light to handle and carry, and so are ideal for those who find lifting heavy leather saddles difficult; they are also easy to clean (you simply wash them down). However, they do not have the lasting qualities of leather saddles; and where some riders find the non-slip seat more secure, others find that it impedes freedom of movement.

Stirrup treads on irons help give the feet a secure, non-slip foothold.

Reins can be plain, laced, rubber, nylon or Continental and should be chosen as carefully as saddles. Thick reins and small hands do not go together, neither do thin reins and large hands. The width and type of rein you choose should feel comfortable when held.

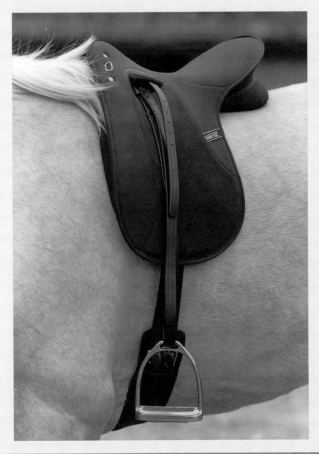

■ Synthetic saddles have the advantages of being light to carry and handle, as well as being easy to care for; you simply brush them off and wash them down when they get filthy!

Health Problems

If a health problem occurs when you take up riding, do not ignore it. Pain felt in joints or muscles, may be caused by a strain, but if it does not clear up after a few days or so, consult your doctor or an experienced sports therapist who specialises in riding. Continuing to ride may cause further stress on the area and could worsen ailments, so until you have found out what exactly is wrong, don't carry on. Pain is a valuable warning sign! Also certain ailments and conditions can be aggravated by riding, so your doctor should be consulted if you are thinking of taking it up and have a disability, or are wanting to continue the sport after an injury. In these cases it helps if you can find a doctor who has a good knowledge of sports injuries (especially riding in your case) and how to treat them.

On the other hand, riding can be therapeutic and help to keep you fit and supple providing any long-standing health problems are taken into account. Many disabled riders have benefitted from riding in one form or another.

The Alexander Technique

Many riders who have suffered pain whilst riding – as well as others who have not – have benefitted from Alexander technique lessons, both on and off the horse. The technique is a method of improving posture and movement, based on the idea that there are right and wrong ways of sitting, standing and moving which will vary according to the individual. It requires the spine and neck to be kept straight, and has been found to help improve both physical and mental health. It is essential, however, that lessons are given by an experienced and qualified instructor if you are to gain benefit from them.

Allergies

Respiratory ailments: A horsey environment inevitably means an atmosphere laden with dust spores from hay, straw and dirt as well as hairs, all of which are conducive to, or will aggravate respiratory problems. If you take up riding but then find that you suffer difficulty in breathing, you should consult your doctor immediately; left untreated, these problems may worsen, and in severe cases may even be fatal. With a known allergy to horses or their environment, taking prescribed medicines and/or wearing a nose/mouth mask can lessen or prevent breathing problems.

Avoid riding in a dusty arena, as this can provoke a severe asthmatic attack if you are sensitive to dust. Throughout the summer or when the weather is mild, ride at dawn or dusk whenever possible when the air does not contain as much pollen.

When grooming, be sure to wear a nose/mouth mask (ask your doctor to recommend something suitable) so that you breathe in filtered air, and if you have your own horse, think about investing in an electric grooming machine with a dust-bag. One famous racehorse trainer found that exposure to certain dusts and vapours around the yard induced an allergic reaction: 'I tried wearing various dust-masks but they were all useless, so then I tried using a rubber respirator. However, that was heavy and uncomfortable.' Eventually he found profound and lasting relief with a 3M respirator. 'Quite simply it changed my life, and I urge other people with respiratory or asthma-related problems to seek advice from medical or environmental consultants.'

The 3M face mask comprises twin elasticated headbands and a bend-to-fit nosepiece to provide a good face-seal; it also features a pre-formed 'off-the-face' design for ease of breathing and speaking. It is thrown away after use.

Always carry medication or your inhaler (if prescribed) with you if you are a confirmed asthmatic.

It is essential that your instructor knows of any respiratory problems you have, so do make her/him aware of them; excitement or anxiety can bring asthma attacks on, so your instructor must understand the importance of not pressurising you unduly to do something that you may be worried about.

Hayfever: Hayfever is an irritation of the nose and eyes caused by grass pollen, and it makes life in summer miserable for riders who suffer from it. Your doctor may recommend a course of desensitisation injections, given in very early spring each year, which reduce and in some cases may even prevent hayfever symptoms.

An alternative treatment lies in taking antihistamine drugs, which again can forestall or even stop hayfever altogether. However, an unfortunate side-effect is very often drowsiness, in which case antihistamines may not be advisable; it will depend on individual reaction. If you do take antihistamines, make your instructor aware so that he/she can teach you accordingly, or administer appropriate first aid if necessary.

Skin allergies: Horses and/or their environment can cause an allergic reaction affecting the skin in some people; these allergies take the form of rashes, itching, raised lumps or pimples. For example, in one case, after riding bareback, the rider suffered a violent reaction to horse sweat and hair in the form of pustulent pimples which covered her thighs and buttocks; these caused excruciating pain. Naturally she avoided riding bareback again, and the problem did not re-occur.

Those who know they suffer from skin problems when riding or being in a horsey environment should consult their doctor, as certain medicines will control allergic reactions. Take the precaution of wearing gloves and long-sleeved shirts to prevent the skin from coming into direct contact with horses or the atmosphere around them.

Some skin allergies do respond to antihistamines, so ask your doctor about these; although you must appreciate that these drugs can cause drowsiness – if you take them, tell your instructor so that she/he is aware.

Back Problems

The health problems that riders most commonly tend to acquire are back ailments of one form or another. Riding puts stress on all areas of the body, as do yard chores, with the back taking the most punishment. The most frequent and common back problems are associated with the sacro-ileac joints between the spine and the hips; these may be caused through strain; sciatica, which is pain in the lower back spreading into the buttocks, thigh and leg, the result of abnormal pressure on the sciatic nerve which runs from the lower back down the legs – it often arises from untreated muscle strains and other back injuries; and joint or muscle inflammation, loosely termed as rheumatism.

In more serious cases after an injury, osteoarthritis can set in; this is a degenerative joint disease where the protective shock-absorbing cartilage between the bones of a joint is worn away.

Never put up with back pain: harass your doctor until you find out what exactly is causing it, and avoid doing things which seem to make the condition worse when you ride, until it has been diagnosed.

In one instance it took a rider ten years of pestering her own doctor and others, to find out what was causing her excruciating back pain, pain which was thought to have been caused by a bad fall. In fact it was not the fall that had initiated the pain, but the effect of it which had aggravated a congenital displaced hip condition; and it was stress to that area brought on by continued riding that brought the condition to her notice. However, as long as she was careful not to place undue stress on that area by adjusting position, the back pain diminished. At least the knowledge that riding wasn't worsening the condition brought some comfort!

One important proviso for back sufferers: make sure you have a horse that *you* find comfortable to ride, so that riding is as smooth as possible.

Avoiding Injury

Many riding injuries can be avoided if the correct preventative measures are taken and silly risks avoided. Wearing and using the right equipment is most important, as is being fit enough to cope with the bodily demands that riding imposes.

Professional instruction is a must, as a qualified and experienced instructor will teach her pupils to ride correctly, taking into account their individual needs. Badly trained or inexperienced instructors may teach faulty techniques that will not only be hard to get rid of, but will also place unnecessary strains on the body.

You can help prevent injury to yourself in two stages: first of all by having proper fitness training (unmounted) to accustom and exercise your body to the level needed for the activities you intend to do when mounted; and secondly, through careful preparation before you ride or take part in a competition (that is, warming up thoroughly).

Your level of fitness rests on four factors: strength, stamina, skill and suppleness. The fitter you are, the less likely you are to incur injury as training will strengthen muscles and tendons so they are able to withstand greater strain imposed on them; it will also strengthen vulnerable parts of the body, such as the back, against pulls and tears. It is important to develop your strength and suppleness equally on both sides of your body – hence the reason you should do an equal amount of work on each rein. The same principle applies to horses!

The more you ride, the fitter you will become; though take care not to over-do riding sessions, as many accidents and injuries occur when you are tired and become careless. However, as you become more skilled, you are less likely to incur injury as you will be able to co-ordinate and control your movements carefully, and will therefore not put undue strain on your body.

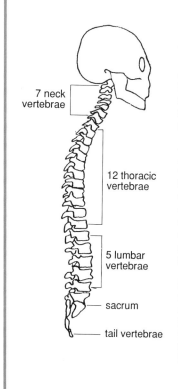

7 neck vertebrae

12 thoracic vertebrae

5 lumbar vertebrae

sacrum

tail vertebrae

■ The human spine is a complex structure. You wonder how on earth it can cope with the enormous stresses we impose on it. The fact is it cannot, which is why you must take particular precautions to exercise safely and within your limits – fittening your body gradually to enable muscles to develop and strengthen correctly so that delicate areas will be protected

Spinal vertebrae are joined together via muscles, discs between the vertebrae and ligaments. Undue strain on the spine can force the gaps between vertebrae to widen, allowing the discs to slip out and become trapped as the vertebrae close back when pressure is relaxed. That's how slipped discs are caused

Movable joints, such as the knee, are supported by ligaments and moved, or partially moved, by muscles. Undue stress on these muscles or ligaments can cause sprain or strain – or even dislocation!

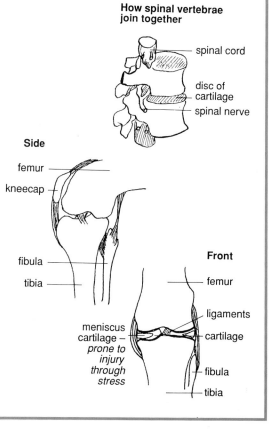

How spinal vertebrae join together

spinal cord

disc of cartilage

spinal nerve

Side

femur

kneecap

fibula

tibia

Front

femur

ligaments

cartilage

fibula

tibia

meniscus cartilage – *prone to injury through stress*

Suppling Exercises

For those who only ride weekly, it pays to exercise at home between lessons to keep supple – especially as you get older. Riding muscles in the legs and back will be less likely to tear if you make them more elastic by gently and slowly stretching them ten or twenty times before putting them under riding strain. Your riding instructor should suggest useful exercises, both on the horse and to practise at home.

As warming up before exercise is important, so too is winding down after it. To help avoid stiffening up after riding, keep gently on the move to prevent muscle-fibre fluid build-up caused by small tears. And rather

■ A lack of body tone and suppleness is the enemy of all riders. Help yourself (and your horse) to better, more comfortable riding by exercising for 10 minutes a day to loosen and fitten you up. Twisting at the waist will help tone and strengthen this area

■ Lengthen and strengthen your back lower leg muscles by standing with your toes, as shown, on a stair or solid box. Let your heels drop down as far as is comfortable, then raise and lower yourself. Start off doing this five times, and work up to ten and then twenty times

■ To strengthen the inside thigh and calf muscles, squeeze a football between your legs at thigh and calf points

■ This a great exercise for stretching, lengthening and toning your inside thigh (riding) muscles! Stand with your legs approximately a yard apart. Then lean your hips to one side, bending the leg on that side forward at the knee to allow you to stretch the other leg down. Keep your upper body square and upright as you do this. Gradually, as you become more supple the further down you'll be able to go!

than having a soak in a hot bath (the traditional remedy after a hard day in the saddle!), have a quick hot or cold shower followed by a brisk towelling down to disperse and re-absorb muscle fluid.

It must be said that if riders knew how the body was constructed, they would almost certainly be more careful in how they used their own, and would take the precaution of warming up before exercise. Like any delicate and precise instrument, it needs to be taken care of and used correctly or it will break. (See Chapter 3 for diagrams of the human skeletal and muscle structures.)

Human bones are pliable structures which have a certain amount of elasticity and properties of compression resistance and tension. They are interconnected by joints, and there is a great variation in the shape and mobility of these joints and in their ability to perform particular functions or exercises. For instance, what one person may be able to do in the way of suppleness, another may not be able to do as easily. A good instructor will be aware of this.

The more mobile joints are supported by ligaments and are moved, or partly moved, by muscles. Undue stress on these muscles or ligaments can cause strain or sprain. Less mobile joints such as spinal vertebrae are held together by discs of shock-absorbing cartilage, which under extreme shock or pressure, such as in the event of a fall, can become displaced and result in what is known as a 'slipped disc'.

Freely mobile joints such as the knees and elbows, hold the bones together by a fibrous capsule which contains a lubricating fluid.

Making Riding Life Easier

Ensure that you only lift what is easily within your own capabilities, and always bend at the knees to lift things, never bend over with straight legs to lift heavy items.

Either make or invest in a mounting block if you have difficulty mounting your horse due to a disability or other body pains. Not only will it save you pain and trouble, it will also save your horse's back and saddle from undue stress.

Avoid over-using a painful area whenever possible. If agreed by your doctor, pain relief can be obtained from a suitable painkiller.

Saddle Sores

Occasionally riders (of either sex) may suffer excrutiating pain in the crotch or buttocks (or both) –

■ As they take part in such a strenuous sport, many horsey people suffer from bad backs. However, part of the problem lies in not knowing how to lift and carry yard equipment correctly to minimise injury. The top photograph shows the wrong way to lift – the vulnerable back is taking all the strain. A classic way to slip a disc!

■ The second view shows the correct and safe way to lift weights, with the legs better positioned to take most of the lifting strain

even to the extent that bleeding occurs. The first course of action is to consult a doctor to ensure there is nothing seriously wrong in these parts to cause such pain. If there is not, then the second course of action is to find out exactly what is causing the pain you suffer when you ride, and so eliminate it. This can be done in several ways:

Position   How you sit in a saddle has great bearing on whether you are comfortable or not.

Saddle   It is important to ride in a saddle that fits both you and your horse correctly and comfortably. It is also essential to sit correctly on the seatbones, not the crotch. Experiment with different saddle types, twist widths and seat depths to find one that feels right. Some women find that a wide twist is the solution to comfort problems, whilst men find the opposite works for them.

A good riding school should match the saddles to the rider wherever possible. If, as a riding-school client, you find your saddle uncomfortable, you are quite within your rights to ask for a different one until you find one that fits you. Nothing is more off-putting to 'new' riders than to feel uncomfortable 'down below' – certainly it does nothing to improve either position or enjoyment if you are gritting your teeth and tensing up to avoid discomfort.

Protection   There are many products available to make life more comfortable, without being too obvious. For example leggings with a padded seat can be worn under breeches or jodhpurs; these are a boon to many people, especially those without the benefit of

a well-covered behind! Men seem to find them particularly helpful. Or you might invest in a seat-saver, a padded saddle-cover that is positioned on top of the saddle – choose one the same colour (dark brown) for unobtrusiveness. If you don't have your own horse and are riding at a riding school, either ask if you can be provided with a seat-saver or take your own to use. Real sheepskin ones tend to be the most luxurious.

For males, wearing a jockstrap as well can provide much-needed relief and support.

Clothing should be chosen with comfort in mind: pick items that feel like a second skin, but that you can also move around in easily. The equestrian clothing market has improved in leaps and bounds in recent years, so finding clothing that is both easy to wear and smart too should never be a problem, whatever your shape and size.

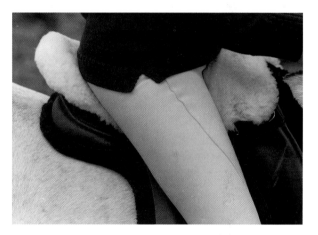

▪ For those whose seats suffer when riding, a cushioning seat-saver can be a real boon

Insurance

It is a very good idea for riders to take out personal accident insurance: riding is a risky sport and however careful you and your instructor are, accidents that are nobody's fault can and do happen. Horses are living creatures and therefore unpredictable. It is advisable to take out insurance against loss of life and earnings, dental bills, medical treatment and equipment loss or damage.

Choose your policy with great care and remember that you invariably get what you pay for: beware, therefore of any companies that offer insurance at

cheaper rates than any other company. Cheap premiums can turn into costly mistakes if the company has 'escape' clauses that cover every eventuality, and you could lose out in the end.

Go through the policy details with a fine toothcomb, and before you commit yourself to paying a premium, satisfy yourself that the company will deal honourably with you in the event of a claim.

If you own a horse, take out third-party and public liability cover – huge bills can soon mount up for damage caused if horses run amok!

THE POSITIVE RIDING MIND AND ATTITUDE

Being a successful rider at any level requires not only physical application but mental talents, too: that is, not your intelligence, but your attitude and how you use your mind. Many riders walk the course at the world-famous Badminton Horse Trials and dream of competing there. Most people carry on dreaming and waiting – and they go back year after year as spectators, still dreaming and still no closer to driving in there as a competitor.

Some years ago one young girl was also there as a spectator, but she was determined to make her dream come true . . . she struggled to reach perfection in all she did, she overcame nasty falls, at one point she almost lost an arm . . . yet still she kept going. That young girl's name was Virginia Holgate, now Elliot, and internationally famous as a top event rider and an Olympiad. Obviously talent has played a part in her success . . . but so has sheer hard work and determination. And in reaching the top Ginny, like many other riders, has also used her mind to the full.

A positive mental attitude is essential to riding, and if you compete, to success (or otherwise); people unwittingly put themselves into a loser's role just by how they think. Try our quick quiz and see how you fare.

1 Your dream is to ride in a Novice horse trials and you are talking about this to a horsey friend. Would you say:
a I wish I could ride in a one-day event.
b I want to ride in a one-day event.

2 You are having a lesson and things are not going too well. On the way home from your lesson you are thinking about the past hour. Which of these sounds the most like you?
a What on earth's the matter with me? Every time I ask for that particular transition I lean forward even though I know it's the wrong thing to do. I must be so stupid. When will I ever get it right?
b I know I've made these mistakes before and today I allowed myself to get really flustered. Next time I'm going to ask my instructor if we can concentrate on those exercises again and I'm going to get it right. I know what to do to get the transition properly and I'm going to rehearse it in my head for a short time every day until my next lesson.

3 Recently you have suffered a dent to your confidence and when show jumping in public you find yourself freezing so you fail to give your horse any instructions. For your next public outing, as you go into the ring, will you think:

a Everything's going to be okay, it'll all be over shortly and then I can go home.
b From the second I go into the ring I'm going to think 'Legs, legs' and make sure I keep using them all the way round.

4 Work commitments mean that you have had to rush to your lesson. Do you:
a Sling the tack on your horse and ride into the arena still thinking about a problem at work.
b Take a few seconds in the stable or trailer to breathe deeply, calm your nerves and switch your mind over to riding matters.

5 You are riding an important dressage test. Do you:
a Ensure that before the big day you have seen videos of a favourite dressage rider and then, just before you go in for your test, imagine you are that rider.
b Work on your own, relying on your feel and experience to tell you how things are looking.

Analysis

Q1: The sort of person who says he *wants* to ride in a one-day event is more likely to succeed than someone who just 'wishes'. Learning the art of riding properly requires a great deal of motivation so you need to set yourself clearly defined, achievable targets. Thus by saying you want to take part in a one-day event, you are making a statement of intent which can then be followed up with a plan on how to achieve it.

Keeping a dream as a wish means it remains as an abstract idea and protects you from the hard reality of doing anything about it! This is an easy way out.

'If you want something hard enough you'll get it' is a well known phrase. Many people have proved this to be the case. Are you a 'want' person and therefore a doer? Or do you prefer the comfortable, secure surroundings of wishing only?

Q2: We all know about the inner voice in our head which berates us when things go wrong – it's very evident in answer a. That voice may have been telling you off for years, reinforcing the idea that you're a slow learner, can't cope with figures, are hopeless at foreign languages and so on. It probably has a field day with your riding, too, sowing seeds of doubt which eventually grow so big that you wonder why you bother getting on a horse at all! However, the attitude shown in answer b demonstrates how that nagging little voice can be silenced! Okay, so you've made a mistake, but everyone does and mistakes can be corrected – you can learn how to do things the right way; all it takes is a little practice. Don't worry about something which has already happened; rather, apply your experience and knowledge so that the mistake doesn't happen again.

One technique which is very useful is that of mental rehearsal (see page 46).

Q3: Facing up to a problem is the only way to resolve it – try to hide it and it's bound to rear its head at some point in the future. Better to turn a problem into an opportunity; look at it differently and you're on the way to cracking it.

Losing your confidence is not a pleasant experience and it's an uphill struggle to regain faith in yourself or your horse. But it's also a valuable exercise to show how determined and single-minded you can be! The approach in answer a only half addresses the problem – basically it's a 'hope-for-the-best' attitude – whereas answer b has a structured method to achieve the goal.

By focusing on something specific which

will help produce a good round, there's more chance of success. Decide on what you want to achieve and then concentrate on it – and this can be applied whenever you school a horse or compete. It also keeps your attention in the present rather than allowing your mind to wander.

Q4: Riding demands 100 per cent concentration, effort and commitment from you, so it's far more profitable to adopt the approach in answer b. It is vital for your riding that you are relaxed, but it is impossible to achieve this state if you are still pondering over hassles at work or home. Before you ride, clear your mind of all distractions – some people imagine standing under a shower and letting all the worries wash away: choose whatever imagery works for you, but make sure you employ it!

Q5: If you adopt answer b you may perform a reasonable test. However, learn to use techniques such as mental rehearsal and visualisation and you can improve even more. Just by pretending that you are Jennie Loriston-Clark, Emile Faurie or some other top rider will have its effect: try it on a friend and see how they automatically sit up and look better.

So, are you a winner or a loser? If it is the latter, don't sink into a pit of apathy! People learn to be losers . . . and they can also learn to be winners. You can harness your mental power to great use, not only in your riding but in other aspects of life, too. All of us are 'less-than-perfect' riders, and for all of us there is a terrific opportunity to improve. Let's take some of the ideas put forward in the quiz and apply them.

THE **POSITIVE** RIDING MIND AND ATTITUDE

1 Recognise what you want and plan how you're going to achieve it. For instance, if your riding ambition is to take part in a Preliminary dressage test, your plan of action may include these points:

a Buy copies of the Preliminary tests so you know the movements required.

b Find a good instructor in your area whose special interest is dressage; explain your goal and ask her/him to help you with a training plan. Have regular lessons with this person.

c Incorporate lessons and regular schooling sessions into your horse's weekly work programme.

d Look out for dressage competitions in your area – go along to watch and learn from other people.

e In conjunction with your instructor, find a competition which would be a good one for you to attend – then you can aim towards a specific date.

f Look out for dressage courses and visiting instructors who may be able to broaden your knowledge.

The advantage of working like this is that you have a structured programme and a clear objective, and you are making the most of resources. People who apply their minds like this are more likely to reach their goals – they plan, prepare, ask questions, try things out and learn from experience. They are also able to cope better when things do *not* run quite to plan. If something is worth doing then it will take considerable effort and there will be times when you feel down; but problems do not seem so bad when you've already worked out options and contingency plans.

The will to learn and the ability to learn from criticism are valuable tools in the struggle to improve your riding. Listen, learn, don't take anything for granted, and be determined to stick at your ambition. Avoid being side-tracked or you'll never make much progress in the right direction.

2 Be kind to yourself We all suffer from the inner voice syndrome evident in Question 2 of our quiz. In addition, you will always hear certain people putting themselves down, for example, when they say 'It's only me' or 'I'm hopeless at . . .' However, why undermine your self-esteem in this way? You are not only affecting how you see yourself, you are presenting a negative image of yourself to other people. In addition, your horse will pick up on this, too! People who lack self-esteem and confidence show this in their body language, which horses can read – and if *you* are unsure about yourself, how can you expect a horse to trust you?!

Build up your confidence by being easier on yourself. Perhaps you couldn't master shoulder-in the first time you tried it, but that doesn't mean you are incapable! You'd be an impressive rider if you *did* grasp everything first time. Besides, everyone has different learning abilities, with some people taking longer to absorb new facts or skills than others. Anyway, it might not be wise to think in terms of competing against other people – you have enough to cope with trying to get your own head and body into shape!

When you do achieve a goal, such as getting a transition right, then you should be pleased with yourself. Make each step forward a pleasant experience and you'll start to feel much more confident.

3 Mental rehearsal To assist in overcoming difficulties, use the mental rehearsal technique. Many top riders, in all equestrian disciplines, use this technique – after all, they have just as many niggly worries when faced with the Lexington cross-country or a puissance wall as you have going round smaller courses. They are humans too, but they have learnt to put their mental powers to good use.

Perhaps you're riding your first cross-country course. You will have walked the course so you are prepared – you know the route exactly, what problems may be encountered, and what to do about them. Do you now just turn up and hope for the best? Why not have a mental rehearsal? Run through the course in your mind – do you ride a perfect round, or do you concentrate on things going wrong?

Used correctly, mental rehearsal is an effective aid for riders. It's rather like playing a video in your head – but as you are the star and the director, you can control the content

of the video. Thus, either you can imagine yourself riding up to the first fence positively, looking ahead, using your legs and sailing over . . . *Or* you can see yourself riding up to the fence, freezing and your horse slithering to a halt because his rider is not giving instructions.

Naturally the first 'vision' will be much more effective, especially if you ride the whole course in your head in this way. You might want to consider difficulties in your run-through, which is fine provided you also consider how, for instance, to deal with a stop, but in a positive way. Then you re-run the video in your head so your lasting impression is one of success!

Visualising yourself tackling a course successfully does have a positive effect on your riding, whilst planning how you would deal with difficulties removes some of the 'fear of the unknown'. All in all you are better prepared, so when the time comes to ride, you can concentrate on the job in hand with a greater measure of self-confidence than if you go in 'cold'.

4 Face up to your fears   At some point in their careers all riders will be afraid, or anxious, or apprehensive about something: to have doubts is quite normal, as is thinking that the odds are sometimes against you – as also is letting those fears get out of perspective. Perhaps you were frightened of things as a child, such as the dark, thunder or spiders; though as an adult you have no doubt realised that these childhood monsters are really not that horrendous.

So why not adopt the same attitude to your 'riding' fears? Look them in the eye and start controlling them, instead of allowing them to control you, therefore limiting your activities and your enjoyment. It would be tempting to say 'OK, I'll start tomorrow' – but that's not good enough! Don't put off until tomorrow what can be done today: live and do now! You cannot affect the past, so there's little point in re-living that last disastrous dressage test or show-jumping round. However, you *can* alter the present and the future.

Face up to your fear and put it into perspective. Perhaps you're afraid of jumping in public? Why? Is it because you're worried about falling off in front of all those people watching around the show-jumping arena? But, other people fall off in public, and do you think anything derogatory about them because they fell off? Of course not!

Remember too, that our mortality limits the time we have to enjoy our riding: thus would you rather conquer a fear and be a better rider, or will you let a fear take control of *your* life and dictate what you will and will not do?

By meeting fears or problems head-on you realise that firstly, they are not as bad as they seemed, and secondly, choosing to *do* something about a fear gives you more control and extra power to get on with the job in hand. Thus fear can be a great motivational force: you *can* change your attitude and give of your best. Every time you *confront* a fear you will make it less fearsome – until eventually you will remove the fear altogether.

5 Balance   Riding requires balance from your body – and also balance in your mind. Concentrate on your negative aspects and you will become tense which is hardly the best attribute for a rider. Therefore be positive about yourself, acknowledge that you will fail at times but that you can use each 'failure' to learn from, and so progress forwards.

Problems cannot be solved by inactivity; success as a rider, or as anything else, will not come looking for you – essentially it is *your* choice to get going and to keep going, no matter how tough it may be.

Key Points

■ Train your mind to work with you, not against you.
■ Train yourself to see fear/obstacles as forces to be mobilised and used in your favour.
■ Recognise that the road to improvement may not be smooth – it isn't for anyone – but it is an infinitely more exciting journey than walking the same path over and over again.

3
THE BODY BEAUTIFUL

No matter what shape a 'natural' rider is, he will always be at one with his horse, will know and anticipate its moods and movements, and will always 'gel' with it. There are very few natural riders, and the majority of horsemen and women find they have to work at achieving 'feel' and correct technique – it would not come easily to them otherwise. However, they may take heart in the knowledge that Lucinda Green, that great horsewoman and superb three-day eventer, does not consider herself a natural, and says that she has to work hard to achieve what she has. To many this statement may seem hard to believe, since very few could ever achieve the heights that she has! But knowing that Lucinda is not a 'natural' rider should give immense and real hope to lesser mortals, those who feel overwhelmed by the struggle to perfect their riding ability and technique.

The Equine Shape

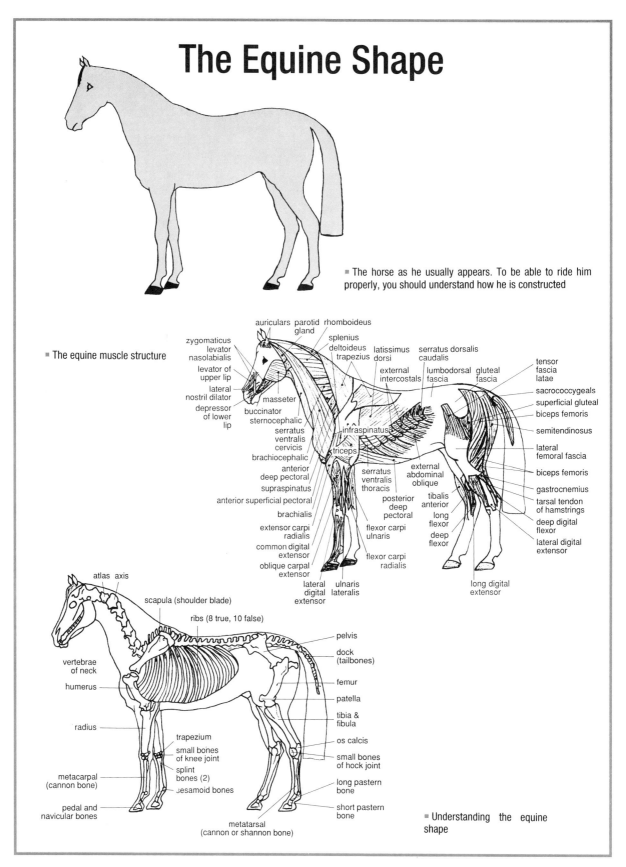

■ The horse as he usually appears. To be able to ride him properly, you should understand how he is constructed

■ The equine muscle structure

■ Understanding the equine shape

The Horse's Structure

It is important to understand how the horse is constructed and moves naturally without a rider, as this has great bearing on how the rider must adapt her/his particular shape to be able to ride comfortably and successfully. If you do not recognise this, you cannot hope to enable both you and your horse to get the most from riding and pursuing your chosen discipline, whether it be simply hacking out, or aiming for the heady heights of three-day eventing. Indeed a caring, thinking rider will first establish how he can adapt himself, both in mind and in body position, to get the best from, and present as insignificant a burden as possible for, his particular horse.

Many riders may not realise that the horse was never designed, structurally, to carry a person; it is only through Man utilising him to carry loads, a tradition originating in Prehistoric times, that riding for pleasure, and for personal gain, eventually came about.

Make it of paramount importance to learn how the horse is put together, then you can understand how best to position yourself – bearing in mind your own shape – so you can ride all horses to their, and your, best advantage. Regarding the horse's structure, he is better able to carry a load of equal proportions spread either side of his spine, resting over his ribs and below, than a load placed directly above him which would rest upon his delicate spine. This is because of the way his muscles, tendons, ligaments and cartilage are structured around his skeleton.

The equine structure is such that a horse cannot easily bend his spine from the base of his neck backwards. It is only by particular muscle strength and tone, achieved through correct schooling, that a horse can 'flex' in the direction required with a rider on board, and carry that rider without strain and stress to himself.

Think of the horse as being an old-fashioned set of scales; if the weight is heavier on one side than the other, the scales will tip in the heavier direction. Now think of yourself as the weights put on those scales, and you will appreciate why it is so important to keep your weight equal on either side of the horse. It is for this reason, too, that saddles have been developed over the ages to help equalise a rider's weight over both sides of a horse and to keep direct weight off the spine. Finding a good saddle that fits both horse and rider comfortably is therefore of paramount importance. You may scrimp on other less essential items, but your saddle is the one thing you have to be prepared to spend most time and money on, to find the right one.

A saddle that fits your horse perfectly, but doesn't fit you as well, is useless as it will not spread the load of your weight correctly once you are on board – this is the reason for many long-term back and behavioural problems found in horses. A saddler who specialises in fitting good quality saddles to people and their horses is invaluable: find one and use him!

Equine conformation differs slightly in each individual according to the vagaries of its breeding, so you must take this into account when buying a horse. Some may have long backs, whilst others are ewe-necked, heavily built, weedy or drastically cow-hocked. Each will need particular training and a good riding technique to make it suitable for your requirements.

First, however, you must identify your *own* build and its particular weaknesses, before you select your horse. And if your shape does not concur with that of a particular horse, it will propably result in an unstable marriage!

Weight-carrying Capacity

The height and build of a horse or pony does not determine what weight it can carry: this is largely determined by how much 'bone' the animal has, the term 'bone' describing the measurement, taken in inches, around the cannon bone just under the horse's knee. As a rough guide, a horse having 8in of bone should be able to carry 154–168lbs (70–76kg), a horse with 9in will be up to 182–196lbs (82–88kg) and a horse with 10–11in of bone will be up to 210lbs (94kg) and more.

However, these approximations are relative as much also depends on the horse's conformation and his bone density; conformation imperfections, for example being back at the knee, can greatly weaken the horse's capacity for carrying weight. Further, even if a horse has 10in of bone, if that bone structure isn't dense, the horse will only be up to around 168lbs (76kg). Remember the old adage 'A pint of blood is worth an inch of bone!' Horses with a good deal of Arabian or Thoroughbred blood in them tend to have greater bone density and strength than more commonly-bred equines, even though their bone measurement may be less.

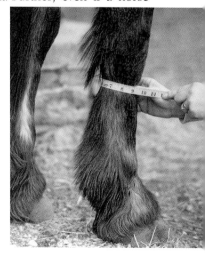

The Human Shape

What is the perfect shape to be able to ride well? Most instructors would agree that a person of willowy conformation with long slim legs and of an ideal weight for his/her frame is best suited to riding horses. This shape looks the most elegant, with the rider having the benefit of plenty of leg length both for security in the saddle and so as to give leg aids with ease. British dressage rider Anni MacDonald-Hall is an excellent example of this shape – but then she is an ex-model, after all!

If you look around, however, you will find that riders blessed with the 'ideal' shape are somewhat thin on the ground. People have to make the best of what they've got – and most do it happily and with considerable aplomb, too! Moreover, look at the shapes of some of the leading riders: they are far from perfect, but it hasn't stopped them from rising to the top of their chosen spheres. Show jumpers Hugo Simon and Ted Edgar are of the short and round variety, whilst three-day-eventers Mark Todd and Rodney Powell are long, tall and lanky. Both shapes, however, have their own particular drawbacks.

The most unlikely horse-and-rider partnership can reach the top, too: Hugo Simon rode the huge, strapping Flipper to great success, and the unbeatable partnership of the diminutive 15.3hh Charisma and the 6ft 4in Mark Todd received worldwide acclaim in the sport of horse trials.

If you look in books and magazines and compare your conformation with others, you may suddenly find that you become more than happy with your shape, and wonder why you ever thought you had problems! Really, there is no such thing as the ideal shape for riding. What there is, however, is the ideal riding mind and attitude – but that's another story and one which you will find in the previous chapter.

Key to Successful Riding

In order to improve your riding ability you must learn to recognise your body shape and how to use it to the best advantage. You will often find weak areas, but you must resolve to work harder to improve these so that your all-round ability improves and suits your horse. Your shape will affect your position and the way your horse goes, so it is equally important to find the right sort and build of horse to complement you and your riding technique. For example a short, tubby person would look out of place and probably feel insecure on a tall, lightweight type of horse, and a tall, thin rider would feel awkward on a smallish animal. A smaller, more substantial animal would suit the former, whilst a taller, bigger-boned horse would feel and look more comfortable for the latter rider. However, riders with short, round legs often find that they cannot sit on a chunkily-built horse comfortably, as they have difficulty in getting their legs around the sides of this sort of animal.

For the purposes of this study we will not consider professional riders, as their talents are in a different class altogether, where often the most unusual horse-and-rider combinations have monumental success, as already mentioned. Such riders have more experience in their little finger than the average horse-owner and rider is ever likely to have in their whole body!

■ This 5ft 11in rider is obviously too tall for this 15.1hh horse. Although the mare can carry the rider's weight easily enough, the rider feels under-horsed and cannot adapt her shape to ride the horse comfortably and effectively

■ *Top right:* A classic case of over-horsing. There is no way this 5ft 3in rider could control this big, strapping 17.3hh chap safely and effectively

The human body is a fascinating and complex structure – no two bodies are exactly the same, although every rider must follow certain basic rules to ensure that his/her own body and shape is cared for safely and kept fit for riding. There is a good deal of difference between the sexes, the most obvious one being that men are much stronger than women. This is because almost half their bodyweight is made up of muscle, as opposed to only a third of the female bodyweight; men therefore have the greater muscle-power potential, hence their greater strength and powers of endurance.

On the other hand, women are often the more patient and sympathetic riders. These elements of male and female if brought together would produce a rider of formidable qualities, so ideally, each sex should work towards gaining the attributes of the other: thus women should work at maintaining physical fitness and body tone, whilst male riders should curb impatience and force and instead strive towards a more sympathetic understanding of how the horse thinks and works. In this way, both sexes would be ideally primed to get the best from any horse.

Riding Fitness

The male body is perhaps less well adapted to riding astride a horse, even though traditionally it was the man's place to do so, whilst women, with few exceptions, rode side-saddle. This fact is quite strange when you consider that the male pelvis is slimmer and the delicate reproductive organs are situated outside the body unprotected from the saddle, whilst the female pelvis is wider, therefore better designed to sit astride a horse, with the reproductive organs tucked safely away inside! Nevertheless both sexes have adapted well to

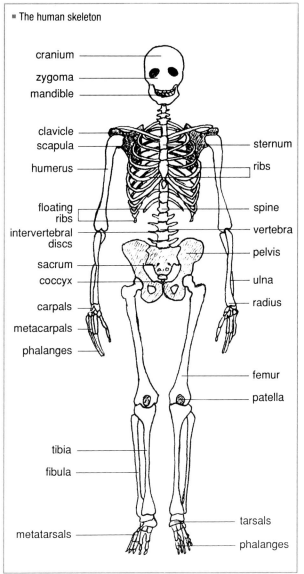

■ The human skeleton

cranium
zygoma
mandible
clavicle
scapula
humerus
floating ribs
intervertebral discs
sacrum
coccyx
carpals
metacarpals
phalanges
tibia
fibula
metatarsals

sternum
ribs
spine
vertebra
pelvis
ulna
radius
femur
patella
tarsals
phalanges

■ Men's bodies tend to be more strongly muscled than women's, and so less prone to be 'flabby'; women have to work harder to keep their bodies in trim and well toned

sitting astride a horse, the general conclusion being that personal tone, fitness and position adaptation are of enormous benefit.

A fascinating observation regarding fitness is that human bone can grow thicker and stronger if subjected to extra stresses and strains; this bone change is seen more commonly in riders, athletes and weightlifters. However, do not let this fact lull you into a false sense of security as bones, muscles, ligaments and tendons will not 'fitten' safely unless the rider ensures that the strengthening process is done slowly and carefully, and always within his capabilities. If muscles have not been strengthened and toned correctly and safely, they will not allow joints to flex easily. 'Forcing' joints into extreme movement will put undue stress on tendons,

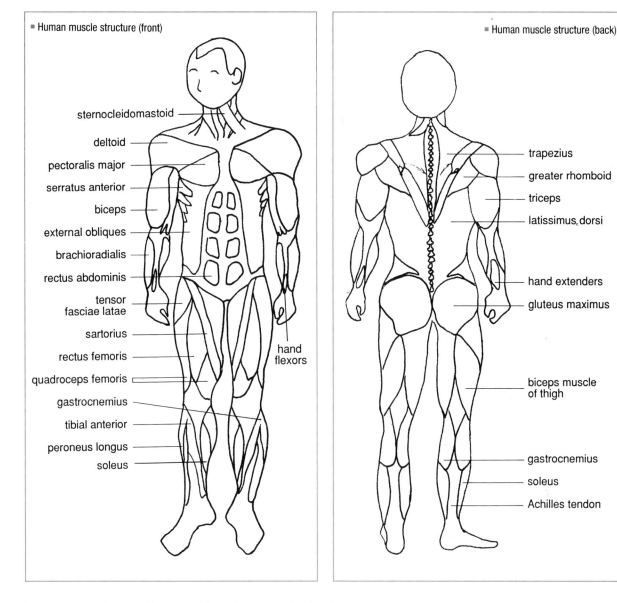

■ Human muscle structure (front)

- sternocleidomastoid
- deltoid
- pectoralis major
- serratus anterior
- biceps
- external obliques
- brachioradialis
- rectus abdominis
- tensor fasciae latae
- sartorius
- rectus femoris
- quadroceps femoris
- gastrocnemius
- tibial anterior
- peroneus longus
- soleus
- hand flexors

■ Human muscle structure (back)

- trapezius
- greater rhomboid
- triceps
- latissimus dorsi
- hand extenders
- gluteus maximus
- biceps muscle of thigh
- gastrocnemius
- soleus
- Achilles tendon

ligaments, cartilage and bones, and put them at real risk of permanent damage.

This system of skeleton and muscles enables us to carry out a wide range of movements and jobs, and is often working when we don't realise it – for example, when we automatically adjust our seat to remain in balance on a horse. This movement involves dozens of muscles and bones which are controlled by the brain.

Any shape can be made to be fit for riding, simply by toning up the body throughout. This toning process starts with the muscles, *before* cardio-vascular fitness can be maintained; only when your muscles are toned correctly for riding can you achieve cardio-vascular fitness as well. The two go hand-in-hand to achieve an overall state of riding fitness the level of which must

be sufficient if you are to ride your horse without stressing him.

Becoming fit to ride gradually and sensibly puts far less stress on your body in the long run; as a consequence you will be less prone, later in life, to injury and other permanent painful and disabling problems. To this end it makes sense to work up to things slowly, and not push your body into doing something it protests painfully about!

Once you recognise what shape your body is, you will be better able to see why certain problems always seem to mar your riding position and technique. Knowing that, you are then better equipped to understand which exercises would be beneficial, and most helpful if you are to beat those riding bugbears!

Pear Shape

Large bottom and heavy thighs

This shape will only affect your riding technique if you let it. It is essential that you keep your bottom, thighs and legs toned up, otherwise loose flab will get in the way of you achieving a deep, secure seat and applying effective and correct leg aids. On the other hand, pear-shaped riders often find it easy to balance (must be the force of gravity!) and establish a comfortable seat (the extra padding comes in handy!).

Common problems encountered by pear-shaped riders:
1 Finding a comfortable saddle to fit their seats without 'overspill'.
2 Difficulty in locating their seatbones, therefore sitting squarely can be a problem.
3 Perching forwards and slouching in an effort to hide a large bottom. This doesn't work – it accentuates a heavy lower half!
4 Difficulty in keeping legs close to the horse's sides, therefore resulting in weak leg aids. This stems from flabby, untoned inside thighs and calves making it impossible to 'mould' legs around the horse.
5 A heavy, unshifting seat, whereby the rider 'cements' himself in place and is not sympathetic to the need for weight adjustment to deliver seat aids. It is a fact that many pear-shaped riders have an 'electric seat', that is, they set their horse alight the minute they mount, due to unsympathetic application of weight!

How this shape affects the horse's way of going:
■ If the rider is not sitting squarely, the horse will react by drifting left or right according to the positioning of the rider's weight instead of moving straight.
■ Perching forwards throws more of the rider's weight on to the horse's forehand, which makes it more difficult for the horse to carry the rider with ease. From a perched, forward position the rider is unable to use weight and legs effectively and so will be unable to ride the horse forwards into a reasonable outline. In addition this perch seat is insecure – if a horse snatched at the reins it could pull the rider further forwards and even more off balance; nor could she/he prevent the horse disappearing into the distance if she/he is always too far forwards.
■ As the rider's legs have only an intermittent contact with the horse's sides, it will probably miss the security of consistent riding. This may be reflected by a generally anxious or unsettled attitude, the ears flicking back and forth and the tail swishing.

Round All Over

A rotund rider often has difficulty in achieving a secure seat and establishing stable balance without becoming 'heavy' and unfeeling. On the plus side, 'round' riders are usually more relaxed than taller, thinner riders, and are therefore less likely to stiffen up. They are also often more sensitive, recognising that they are at a disadvantage as far as shape goes, and strive to be as considerate to the horse as possible.

Common problems faced by rotund riders:
1 Lack of balance.
2 An often unconsciously 'ham-fisted' approach.
3 Finding a horse and saddle that can accommodate their shape, combined with height and weight, comfortably.
4 Recognising and achieving 'feel'.
5 Toning their bodies up effectively to use them to the best advantage.
6 Feeling at a disadvantage from the start by being extremely conscious of their figure.
7 Fending off 'insinuations' or actual insults from riders whose shape is perhaps more ideal.
8 Having the confidence to go out and enjoy their chosen hobby or sport without feeling self-conscious.
9 Finding riding clothes and boots that fit comfortably and look good.

How this shape affects the horse's way of going:
■ Carrying an out-of-balance rider is a real trial for a horse; some more genuine souls manage more easily than others, so the effects on the way the horse moves can be dramatically different. Riding-school horses are often seen plodding along showing little interest in life, whereas other horses will not tolerate a rider who is not particularly balanced, and will drop a shoulder or nip around a turn!

Instead of going forwards enthusiastically and in a relaxed manner, a horse battling with a heavier-than-necessary load on its back will show its displeasure by some form of resistance.
■ Heavy-handed riders can easily upset horses. After all, the horse's mouth is extremely sensitive (or should be, providing it has always been properly ridden), and it will object to roughness by going backwards instead of forwards; tossing its head; grinding its teeth; pulling away or running away from the pain caused by the rider's hands; bucking, or generally trying to get rid of the rider.

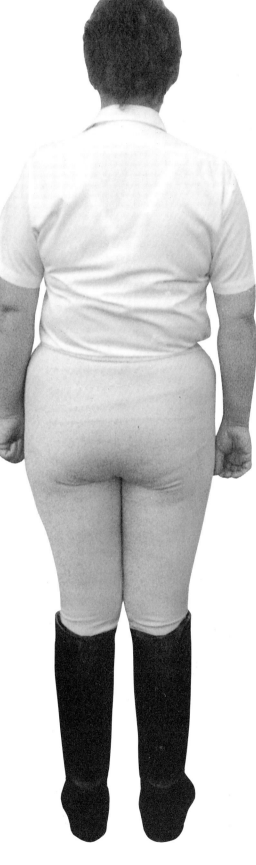

Short Legs, Tall Back.

This shape has perhaps more advantages than other 'less-than-perfect' ones – you can at least work on 'lengthening' your legs to achieve the overall elegant shape that your back promises! However, do not overdo it; some instructors maintain that the only position to have is one where the legs are as long as is physically possible so you achieve the ideal shape *and* give correct and effective leg aids. However, this only works if you are comfortable doing it! In actual fact it makes more sense to ride shorter if it is more effective than to ride in an uncomfortably stretched and therefore useless position!

Common problems faced by short-legged riders:
1 Finding a saddle with comfortable flaps of the right length.
2 Gaining enough strength and 'length' in the legs so they can work effectively.
3 Finding just the right size and build of horse to feel comfortable and be effective on.

How this shape affects the horse's way of going:
■ Particularly if a horse is naturally strong or heavy on its forehand it will be a difficult task for a short-legged rider to create enough impulsion; as a result the horse will tend to go in a long, flat shape, rather than in a round outline with the hindquarters engaged.

The Ideal Shape

Having the 'ideal' shape for riding is all well and good, but it can only be fully effective with the mental approach to match: with both these elements you *do* have a rider to be reckoned with! However, 'imperfect' riders should realise that achieving this equation isn't easy, and that although an ideally-shaped rider has all the advantages of looking good, the crucial test lies in whether that shape will get the best from a horse. And if he/she does not also have the ability to feel at one with a horse and be sympathetic to its temperament and way of going, then he/she will have to work just as hard at becoming a good rider as those with a less-than-perfect shape.

Common problems faced by ideal riders:
1 Those who lack real application to the job; lack of self-confidence; or an over-abundance of confidence, blinding oneself to faults and the realisation that one can improve on one's ability.
2 Failing to work at tone and suppling exercises to maximise riding potential: even blessed with the ideal shape you still have to work at being fit to ride.
In all, to be an ideal shape *and* rider you have to work at it just as hard as those who are less well endowed. The only real advantage you have is the ideal shape to start with.

Effect on the horse's way of going:
■ If the rider can adopt the correct riding position then the horse ought to go well – but of course, even the perfectly shaped rider cannot make a top dressage star out of a choppy striding animal.
■ Any of the problems that other riders face may occur in horses ridden by people with the supposedly ideal shape, because there are far more components to a successful rider than shape alone!

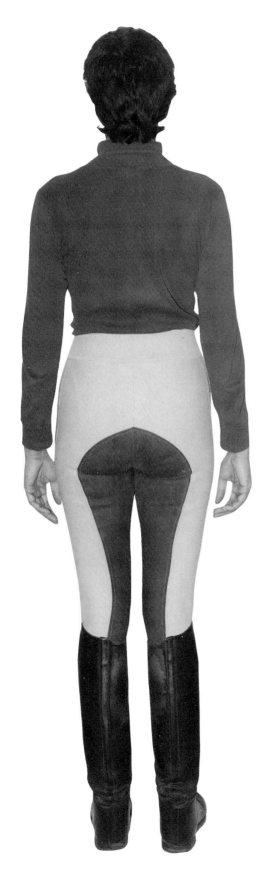

Tall, yet Weight in Proportion to Size

This also could be an 'ideal' shape. Overall, the rider's body is long but it is perfectly in proportion weight-wise. In an ideal situation this sort of shape is desirous as it has the length, conformation and proportionate weight to work effectively and be pleasing to the eye.

Common problems faced by tall riders:
1 Finding a horse of the right height and conformation to suit you.
2 Stiffness, in trying to achieve what is supposed to be the 'correct position'.
3 A somewhat angular position.
4 The inclination to 'hunch up' in an attempt to appear smaller. Tall people tend to be somewhat self-conscious, but since you cannot change your height you may as well be proud of it and make the imposing most of it. Take advantage of what it can offer!

Effect on the horse's way of going:
■ If a tall rider does hunch up, rounding the shoulders and back, then he will not be sitting efficiently so the horse's balance will be affected.
■ In addition, from this position, he is not able to make the best use of his weight aids, which will affect the quality of the instructions he can give to the horse.
■ As they are usually long in the arms too, tall riders do not always fold as far forwards as they should when jumping; when the fences get bigger, this can affect their balance slightly.

Tall, but Thin for Height

Whilst a tall shape is desirable for the sake of elegance, being thin with it can cause a 'stalk' effect if the rider is stiff and unyielding. Taller riders are, for some reason, more rigid than 'well-padded' ones, and the hardest hurdle for them to overcome is simply to relax and become 'at one' with the horse.

The secret of looking 'at one' for these riders is to allow themselves to 'flow' with the horse's movement so they can soften their shape and position. A comparable example to model yourselves upon is Mark Todd.

Common problems faced by riders of this shape:
1 Looking angular and stiff.
2 Feeling comfortable when mounted, as the lack of 'padding' in the seat area can make life extremely uncomfortable.
3 Finding riding clothes to fit, which do not make you look like a stick insect!

Effect on the horse's way of going:
■ Being uncomfortable because of lack of padding when trying to execute sitting trot usually leads to tension and stiffness which may cause the horse to hollow its back against the rider. Hollowed backs are generally accompanied by the horse raising its head and neck and showing other signs of resistance.

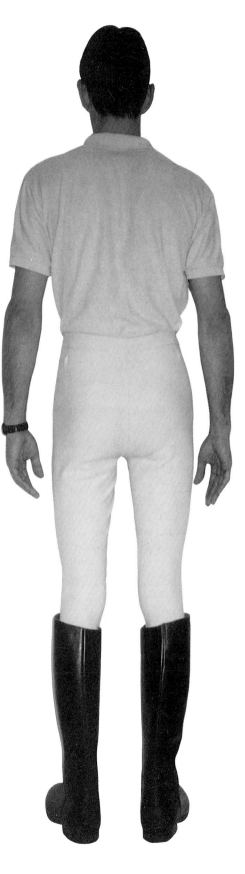

Long Legs, but Short Upper Body

Long legs are an advantage, but a short upper torso can make it difficult to look elegant when mounted. Determination is needed in striving to sit as tall as possible, but without it being uncomfortable and unnatural. This is to create the illusion of tallness to match the reality of the long and shapely legs. Imagine you are riding like an equestrian idol: it can work wonders for your position.

On the ground, many male riders do appear comparatively short in the top half, whilst long from the waist down. Yet mounted, they often present an overall tall and graceful effect.

Common problems faced by riders of this shape:
1 Hunching up: the result of balance, confidence and co-ordination problems.
2 The 'short arm' syndrome. Being short in the torso often means that you have a shorter reach, therefore you feel you must lean forwards to take up and maintain contact. However, you must learn *not* to lean forwards, and to ask the horse to come to you rather than the other way around.

Avoid buying a horse that is long in the back and neck; life will be far more comfortable on a more compact animal.

Effect on the horse's way of going:
■ Hunching up and leaning forwards – this all adds to the weight the horse has to carry on his forehand (see page 56).

Petite

The petite rider, whilst maybe perfectly formed for her size, seems to have the most problems in coming to terms with what size and conformation of horse she is best suited to. Many make the mistake of riding horses that are far too big and strong for them, in the often foolish assumption that they themselves will appear more impressive and able riders.

In some exceptional cases, a small rider and big, strong horse will 'gel'. However, in the case of 'ordinary' riders, remember that the more suited a horse is to your own build and size, the more successful the partnership is likely to be.

Avoiding the 'pea on a drum' appearance is important if you are not to look out of place on a horse, especially if your particular interest is in showing. In these classes it is important to look suited to your horse otherwise the whole effect is ruined.

Common problems faced by petite riders:

1 Feeling comfortable within themselves – that is, knowing their own limits as to the type and size of horse or pony they are best suited to and coming to happy and contented terms with that.

2 Finding a horse that they feel comfortable with and in control on.

Effect on the horse's way of going:

■ Providing the petite rider is suitably mounted and strives to achieve the correct riding position, there is no reason why the animal should not go well for her. Strong animals may present a problem, particularly if the rider is unable to sit tall and use her weight.

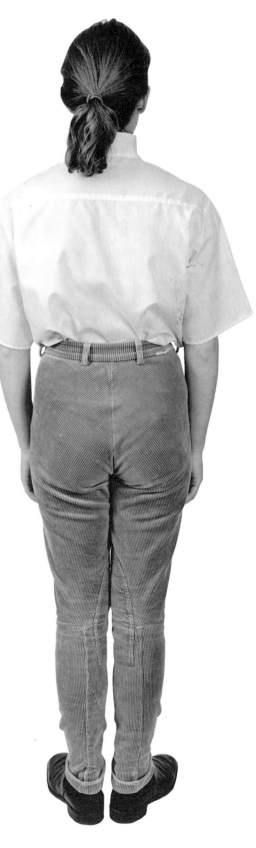

Helpful Exercises

Sitting behind an office desk all day will create more problems with your riding than the fact that you are tall, short or round! Tension and stiffness are the worst enemies of riding, and if you have a somewhat sedentary lifestyle at work it is inevitable that you will not be as supple or toned up as you might like to be. Additional exercises, as well as everyday riding, will help – try and arrange your day to include a 20-minute session incorporating some or all of the dismounted exercises listed below: you will soon feel a difference! Check your diet too.

Remember that initially your unfit body will almost certainly be a little stiff after your exertions – always warm up before and cool down after each workout, and do not push yourself so hard that you are in pain! It is advisable before you start any exercise programme to consult your doctor, especially if you have specific injuries or problems. In addition there are now a number of sports therapists, some of whom specialise in riding. A consultation with an expert will provide you with a programme worked out specifically for you – at no great cost.

The exercises which follow will develop your strength and suppleness, and help your co-ordination.

■ Hunched over a desk all day doesn't help your posture. You have to make an effort to sit correctly.

Dismounted Exercises

Press-ups: Ideal for strengthening your arms, legs and the abdominal muscles – try to keep your back flat.

Touching the toes: Stretches the muscles down the back of your legs and helps with suppleness in the waist area. If you cannot reach at first just go as far as you can – with time you will be able to stretch down further.

Stand and stretch: Good for stretching leg muscles, improving your balance and suppling your waist. Make sure that whatever you rest your foot on is a sensible height for you, as shown here.

Dismounted Exercises

Leg swings: Swing each leg in turn back and up, keeping your leg reasonably straight and without tipping forward. Your upper body needs to remain tall (as it would if you were sitting in the saddle). Only swing your leg back as far as it is possible without causing any pain in your lower back.

Sit-ups: Help to strengthen the stomach and back muscles.

Side leg stretches: Lift your legs out to the side as high as you can, but try to remain square with your upper body. You can see here that our model is leaning in towards the chair. This really stretches all the muscles along the inside of your leg.

Head rolls: Loosens up the neck and shoulder area.

Arm circling: Opens up the shoulder area.

Dismounted Exercises

Splits/toe touching: Stretching down from this position to touch your toes tones up the muscles in your legs and stretches/tones the muscles on the sides of your body.

Splits/stretching forwards: A useful exercise to practise, keeping a flat back for jumping position – note that our model should be looking up so that her back is flat instead of rounded.

Folding: Another useful one to practise, folding from the waist for jumping position – note the arm's position to check that the back is flat.

The chairless exercise: For this exercise stand against a wall, then take a short step away from it, bend your knees and, keeping your back against the wall, sit on an imaginary chair! This helps build the strength in your thigh muscles, but you will soon discover that it's pretty hard work! – Initially you will not be able to hold this position for more than a few seconds.

Hips loosener: Lie on your back and cycle with your legs; lie on your back, stretch your legs out to the side, forwards and back.

Mounted Exercises

These can be performed moving on the lunge, or at a standstill if your horse is held by a reliable person. Be sure to do the same number of repetitions for each leg/arm so that your body is exercised equally.

To loosen up and supple the upper body:
■ Turn your head slowly to the left, then to the right. Roll your head slowly so that you describe a circle.
■ Lift your shoulders up as if you are trying to touch your ears with them, then let them drop down, and relax. Draw your shoulders back as if you are trying to make your shoulder blades touch each other, then relax.
■ Circle your arms backwards, one at a time and then together.
■ Lift your hand to touch your shoulder, then raise your arm up, then back to the shoulder, then arm out to the side and back.

Exercise for the waist and back:
■ Keeping your legs in the correct position, lean forwards from the waist towards the horse's neck, come up and lean back towards the horse's tail.
■ Touch your toes, initially right hand to right toe, then right hand to left toe.
■ Hold your arms out to the side and horizontal to the shoulders, swing your body right and then back to the normal position, left and then back. Do this without moving your legs around and look ahead at all times.

Leg exercises:
■ Gently swing your legs backwards and forwards ensuring that your upper body isn't tipping or leaning excessively.
■ Take hold of your ankle and draw your leg up, pull your leg up so that your ankle is brought closer to your bottom, then relax.
■ Rotate the ankles.

Seatbones:
■ Take hold of the pommel of the saddle with one hand and without leaning back too much, draw up both knees as high as you can so that you can feel your seatbones. Now turn your legs away from the saddle, hold that position for a short while, then relax and let your legs hang down.

Other Activities

■ *Cycling* is a great exercise for improving your leg muscle strength and tone – provided you cycle standing up, of course!
■ *Jogging* helps your breathing (useful for cross-country riding and coping with nerves!).
■ *Swimming* is the best all-round exercise for strength suppleness and stamina.

■ Many DIY horse owners will usually find that they are already quite fit from daily riding and doing all the yard chores. But beware of doing more harm than good as you carry straw bales, buckets of water, push laden wheelbarrows and muck out six months-worth of deep litter bed. It is all too easy to pull muscles and strain backs if you do not carry and lift items correctly.

4

COMMON FAULTS ON THE FLAT

It is a fact that 99.9 times out of a 100, it is the rider who is at fault if a horse does not behave or won't respond to the aids (the method of directing horses what to do and communicating with them). You may imagine that you have given them correctly and clearly, but certainly the success of physical aids depends on how effective your position in the saddle is.

When the horse does actually 'misbehave' he is usually, wrongly, punished. Many a rider, unfortunately, is too quick to blame his or her horse, rather than realise the animal has misbehaved because of something he/she has done, or failed to do, such as given confusing or conflicting aids; or presenting an uncomfortable burden due to a poor position.

This chapter is designed to help you recognise your own riding faults (and you are bound to have some!) and find out what effect they have on your horse so that you may then address them.

The Basic Aids

A rider has four main means of communication and therefore the aids fall into four categories; these are listed below in the order of their importance, although the first three are principle and must be used in conjunction with each other.

The four categories are, mental aids, vocal aids, physical aids and artificial aids.

Artificial aids do have a positive and helpful function, but it is essential that you have a thorough and effective understanding of the first three groups before you consider using them.

The Mental Aids

Mental aids are the most important, as you have to be in a positive frame of mind to get the best both from yourself and your horse (pp 44–7). Stressed and frustrated riders transmit their feelings to their horses and this leads nowhere, except that both parties become extremely unhappy. Nothing is gained if you get wound up with your horse: you should always be able to reprimand him without losing your temper, even if this takes great self-control!

Sometimes it is difficult to know precisely when your horse is 'having you on' and when he genuinely doesn't know what you require of him as he does not understand your aids. Determining which is the case depends upon experience, and the real desire to understand equine behaviour and to use this knowledge correctly.

If you get cross unreasonably and let your horse know it, nothing is gained on either side and the relationship between you can become permanently soured. Besides, if you give a direction and your horse doesn't respond, it is almost certainly because *you* haven't prepared and asked him properly anyway. So before you get tough, question your technique – both mental and physical. Never punish your horse in anger. Calm down, relax, and think positively before you ask something of your horse again. A happy, relaxed outlook on your part will be reflected in the way your horse performs, and a clear head enables you to give clearer and more well-defined signals!

The Vocal Aids

Talking to the horse is a method of communication which is sadly under-used. The voice is a very powerful aid, whether to praise, reprimand, encourage or soothe. The horse quickly learns to interpret your tone of voice and respond accordingly.

No horse likes to be chastised, but they all love being praised so use this fact to your benefit! Many people are shy of talking to their horse whilst riding it – perhaps they think they'll be thought strange if overheard? But what could be stranger than not talking to your partner!

Horses soon learn what a tone of voice conveys when it is used in conjunction with physical aids, and this is why the voice is of great help when schooling a young or 'green' horse. The instructions you give physically might not be understood at first, but if used with vocal aids he'll soon get the idea of what you require from him. Your vocal tone and pitch will indicate what you wish to convey.

The golden rules to follow are:
■ To pitch your voice quietly and on downward tones when you want the horse to slow or calm down;
■ Lift the voice enthusiastically when you want an upward transition or extra effort from him;
■ Use your voice in a sympathetic and reassuring way when you want to encourage him to do something if he's scared;
■ Be sharp and firm if he's being downright naughty or trying to pull a 'fast one'.

Practise using your voice in these ways – some people find it harder to talk to their horse than others and have difficulty in pitching and toning their voices accordingly.

The Physical Aids

These include the use of your balance, weight, seat position, legs and whole bodyweight and your hands (use them in this order): all of which can be used independently or jointly to create the response in your horse that you desire.

It does take time and practice before a rider manages to 'feel', co-ordinate and work each bit of the body independently. Everyone has problems co-ordinating at first (there's so much to remember to do all at once!),

so don't worry if you seem to be struggling on longer than others. However, it's a bit like learning to drive or to ride a bike – everything clicks into place eventually!

A good instructor will be of enormous help to you, but remember that each rider is different, and some find this initial stage easier than others.

The Artificial Aids

Whips, spurs and other items of tack that help the rider control a horse or pass messages to it are all included under the term 'artificial aids'. Certainly they have their place and can be of great help to a rider, but as with anything they have to be used correctly to work effectively, and should not be used to cause distress, fear or pain to the horse. Spurs can in fact be kinder on the horse if they are used to give a gentle, clearer aid – more so than a confusing kick or squeeze. Spurs should only nudge, and not be dug or kicked in.

Schooling whips should be applied behind the rider's lower leg – a flick will reinforce and sharpen the clarity of a leg aid if needed, and the horse will learn to respond to the leg and know what it means, rather than have the whip used more indiscriminately.

■ Artificial aids. *Left to right:* running martingale, schooling whip, jumping whip, spurs and standing martingale.

Starting the Right Way

■ The correct position. The rider is sitting on the horse's centre of gravity; note the line going through her ear, shoulder, hip and heel. Relate this diagram to the picture above

If your position is not correct the horse will find it difficult to carry you, and *you* will find it awkward to give any of the previously explained aids effectively. You will therefore end up sending unclear and confusing messages to your horse. (See Chapter 1 for position guidance and hints.) Finding a comfortable, effective and essentially correct position is probably the hardest thing you will ever have to do as far as riding is concerned, particularly as sometimes you may have to diversify slightly from the 'proper' one to suit your physique.

It is easy to become muddled about what is the right way of sitting on and riding a horse properly, especially if your instructor changes frequently. Also, every horse differs slightly in how it will react to aids; as all riders are individuals and should be treated as such, so are horses, and an aid that one particular horse understands may totally confuse another. Therefore it is worth considering that some horses you ride may not have been schooled to respond to the aids *you* have been taught to give –

again, especially if you change instructors or riding schools. As explained in Chapter 1, although instructors stick mainly to the basic principles when teaching people to ride, they often devise slightly different methods that they have, hopefully, found to work better.

When you ride different horses you must make it your business quickly to establish what directions they identify with, for you can be sure that they will all respond differently in some ways, to a lesser or greater extent. Bear in mind also that you will not au-

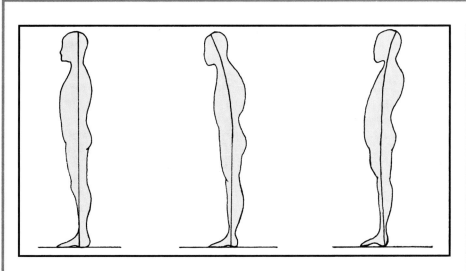

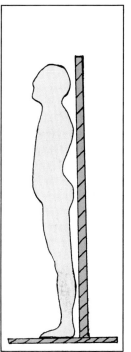

tomatically 'gel' with some horses, though do not take it to heart if this happens – it's like finding friends, some people you get on with and some you don't. However, *you* can choose who your friends are, but horses have to put up with a certain rider or owner, whether they like it or not. In these cases we can only hope that the 'unsuitable' owner/rider will realise that he is not suited to his horse and, rather than persevere and make life miserable for both of them, will sell it on to someone who *can* forge a successful partnership.

All of this may sound somewhat daunting at first! However, to be a sympathetic, successful and caring rider who makes life easier and more enjoyable both for himself and his horse, you must set out to:

1 Find the right sort of position that is both comfortable and effective.
2 Find the right type of horse that you can identify with, and will be able to 'teach' to respond to your techniques easily.
3 Realise what faults you have and cure them: to do this you have to . . .
4 Think hard about how your way of riding affects the way your horse goes and behaves; also how you feel about your own ability, that is how successful you are in getting horses to respond to you positively.

■ To help you feel correct posture, stand against a wall and aim to achieve the position shown in (b)
a) Hollow posture with hips jutting down and out
b) Correct posture with taut abdomen and hips up, back and slightly down to tilt pelvis correctly

■ *Top:* To achieve a good position on a horse, practise correct posture when dismounted, so that it becomes second nature

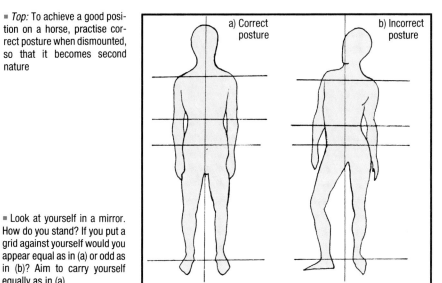

a) Correct posture

b) Incorrect posture

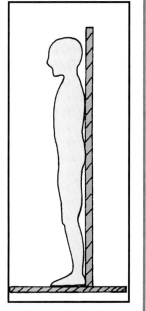

■ Look at yourself in a mirror. How do you stand? If you put a grid against yourself would you appear equal as in (a) or odd as in (b)? Aim to carry yourself equally as in (a)

Back to Basics

Whatever level you are at, there is always room for improvement, and those that think they can ride without having, or feeling the need for regular lessons may well be surprised at the difference a person on the ground makes. Bad habits creep in all too easily, and almost before you realise it, your horse has taken advantage of your faults and is either misbehaving when you ride him, or you find that getting him to do things is no longer as easy as it once was.

Faults in riding style apply both to beginners and to the more experienced. To this end, effecting a 'cure' yourself is simpler if you know what riding faults commonly affect the way horses go, how to diagnose them, and how to overcome them.

This chapter is designed to help you make the most of your lessons or, if you cannot manage to have regular instruction, to give you pointers which will actively help you get to grips with your particular riding problem. However, it must be emphasised that whilst there are plenty of handy hints to help you overcome the riding faults that are hindering you, a complete cure can only arise if *you* are determined enough to beat them for good.

Much depends on the extent to which you can control your mind, and direct it into saying 'I can!', rather than 'I can't!'. Positive thinking has everything to do with success, and must be applied if you want to get anywhere. Caroline Davis, co-author, has never forgotten what a primary school teacher said to her some twenty years ago: in reply to Caroline's 'I can't do this – it's too hard!' she said: 'There's no such word as *can't* in my book – you can do anything you want if you set your mind to it!' A truer statement was never made!

In the end, curing bad habits and finding the solution to particular problems all comes down to your own self-discipline. Without this, you cannot ever hope to achieve what you are aiming for.

Mounting and Dismounting

For beginners, actually getting on and off a horse presents the first problem, since neither is as easy as the experts make it look. However, practice does make perfect, and you'll find that you soon get the hang of it.

Real problems arise when you have difficulty getting on and off a horse for the following reasons:

1 You are small and the horse is large.

2 Physical reasons such as disability, pain, a lack of suppleness.

3 Your horse won't stand still!

Remedies:
- Use a mounting block and teach your horse to stand quietly by it whilst you get on and off him. If you have cause to dis-

mount whilst out hacking, make use of 'natural' mounting blocks in the forms of walls, logs, rocks and so on, both to get off and to remount.

- If you are not supple, try to exercise both on and off the horse, to tone and loosen you up (see Chapter 3 for relevant suggestions and instructions).
- All horses can be taught to stand quietly whilst you get on and off them – it's simply a question of using the right method combined with firmness and patience.

If your horse responds well to your voice, tell him to 'Stand' whilst you mount or dismount. Keeping contact with his mouth on both reins should prevent him walking off – sometimes holding the inside rein shorter than the outside does the trick. With persistent offenders, make them face a wall or fence so they *cannot* go anywhere.

Do ensure that the saddle fits correctly, as a painful back will cause your horse to move around when you mount.

As with everything else, always reward your horse with a kind word and a pat when he does as you require – that way he'll learn which sort of behaviour means reward, and which means chastisement.

■ Rising too high out of the saddle and losing all rein contact. Looking where you are going helps you to balance automatically

■ *Opposite:* Training your horse to stand whilst you make use of a mounting block can be a great help

■ Keep your hips and shoulders parallel to the horse's shoulders so that you move with, not against, him

Learning to Trot

The greatest problem initially which besets the novice rider is getting the hang of trot and canter; when you are learning to ride, staying put in canter can run a close second to rising trot in terms of difficulty! However, first things first, and bouncing about out of rhythm is the main problem the novice rider must solve when the horse starts to trot. Sitting trot tends to bounce you off balance, which leads to you perching forwards in the saddle, gripping up with the legs and unable to guide the horse with quiet and steady hands. In rising trot, the difficulty is getting the hang of exactly when to rise out of the saddle and when to sit again. The rider frequently rises too high and is then left behind the movement, therefore rising out of balance in an uneven rhythm.

Remedy:

Correct instruction on a comfortable, obedient horse with smooth, even paces works wonders. Trotting without stirrups helps the rider achieve 'feel', and teaches him how to move naturally with the horse instead of against him.

The trot is a two-time movement, the horse moving diagonal pairs of legs in order to propel himself forwards. It helps you balance, then learn to rise and sit in rising trot, if you count 'One . . . two . . . One . . . two . . . and so on', out loud (or in your head).

Remaining in a basically correct and comfortable position is the next step. Remember to keep your shoulders parallel to the horse's shoulders, so that when you ride a circle or turn a corner you are going with him and not away from him. Look around your turn or circle too, not fixedly straight in front of you or through the horse's ears (tunnel vision). This will *feel* better for a start, because if you are looking where you are going, your body will automatically adjust its balance accordingly.

Allow your body to soften but without becoming floppy, then the shock of the trot movement will be absorbed and you won't bounce so much. For a closer, more comfortable ride allow your hips to 'roll' with the motion rather then set them against it. To hunch up when you feel unsafe is a perfectly normal reflex action, but it is the worst thing you can do on a horse as you'll be in no position to remain in control or regain balance.

Try to keep yourself relaxed and long a) so that you can move with the horse, and b) so that you have as much leg as possible either side of the horse to help you keep your seat.

Sitting trot: Think of allowing each seatbone to move forwards with each relevant hindleg as the horse brings it underneath you. This takes practice (it also helps if you count in time to the trot beat), and you may feel as though you are 'shimmying' in the saddle to begin with, but you'll soon find it becomes more comfortable. The other advantage of this movement is that you can effectively regulate the speed of the trot.

Rising trot: To be able to do rising trot you need to incline very slightly forwards to remain in balance with the horse. The idea is to sit as the outside foreleg comes back down to the ground, and rise as it goes forwards. This is known as sitting on the correct diagonal. If you were on the wrong diagonal (sitting as the inside foreleg came to the ground) your heavier inside weight would overbalance the horse on turns and circles.

To help you get the hang of sitting on the correct diagonal, watch for when that outside leg comes to the ground and say 'Now . . . Now . . .' when it does. Next, sit when you say 'Now', then rise, and then sit again on the next 'Now'.

If you are on the wrong diagonal it is quite quick and easy to change over – simply sit for two beats instead of one before continuing to rise. Remember to change diagonal when you change the rein. To rise and sit easily and correctly, let the horse 'bounce' you up slightly, then allow your hips and pelvis to go forwards before returning your seat to the saddle.

Don't stand up in your stirrups to rise or you'll end up rising behind the movement. Let your lower legs help you rise, not your knees, or the movement will be jerky. As you become more efficient at rising trot you'll find that your seat will lift itself automatically, so that you will not need to 'lever' yourself up with your legs.

Achieving and maintaining trot: Sometimes the problem is in actually getting into and maintaining the trot. To do both successfully you need to ensure that the preceding walk is of good quality and that the horse is listening to you constantly.

The aids for trot are: Check that you have correct flexion (you should be able to see the corner of your horse's inside eye). Ensure the walk has sufficient impulsion before half-halting – a tiny indication with leg and hand, which should be imperceptible to the eye and warns your mount of an impending gait change; for actual trot, drop the weight slightly more into your seat and squeeze your horse's sides with both lower legs.

Maintain the squeeze as your horse moves off into trot so that he doesn't come back into walk again. Then you can relax your legs, but keep them on his sides both for security in the saddle, to stop them from flapping around, and to maintain impulsion as required.

Learning to Canter

It is vital that a rider's position, confidence, seat and balance are firmly and correctly established before canter is attempted. This is so that should the usual position problems occur initially, the rider is sufficiently well prepared to be able to take the corrective measures in canter that his instructor advises.

Those usual problems are:

1 Finding it hard to make a smooth, controlled transition from trot to canter (either the horse does not have enough impulsion, or goes into a faster trot).
2 Maintaining canter.
3 Perching forwards.
4 Leaning back.
5 Bouncing up and down.

Transitions: Ensure that you maintain impulsion and an even rhythm in trot, so that your horse is able to go up a gait easily and smoothly. Achieving a good transition is dependent on impulsion, on even rhythm, and sufficient preparation beforehand – that is, making sure that you have warned your horse of a forthcoming pace-change by way of a half-halt, plus checking that your position is correct enough to give the required aids clearly.

The aids for canter are: go into sitting trot; inside hand asks for inside flexion; outside rein controls flexion and speed; inside leg remains on the girth to send the horse off into canter on the correct leading leg (unless you want counter-canter!) and to provide support for the horse to 'bend' around; outside leg goes slightly behind the girth to maintain impulsion and prevent the quarters from swinging out.

Initially ask for a canter transition when you are going around a corner, because it is easier for you both to balance. Never persist in trying to push your horse into canter from a speedy trot – this is uncomfortable for you, and you will both be too unbalanced to achieve it. Bring the trot back under control before you ask him again. If you have the same result yet again, make sure that it is not *you* giving unclear or incorrect aids, so causing your horse to 'disobey'. Try once more, and if you are sure you are asking him correctly but he again refuses an instant and correct transition, back up your

aids with a tap behind your inside leg from your schooling whip.

If your horse persists in taking off into an uncontrolled canter, check that it is not your position that is causing him to do so. A heavy, unyielding seat and a forward position will encourage a horse to 'race on'. Sit tall and light, and use half-halts to help steady the horse. Counting the canter beat (one ... two ... three ... and so on) in your head will help you relax back into the required slower, even rhythm.

■ The rider's hands are restraining in canter whilst the legs are not close nor steady on the horse's sides and therefore the rider cannot maintain the horse's impulsion

Maintaining canter: The most usual causes of being unable to maintain the canter are (a) the rider's hands and arms are stiff and unyielding, therefore hampering the horse's forward progress; and (b) lack of impulsion due to insufficient leg contact.

In the case of (a) the rider must realise that the horse's head nods up and down in canter, just as it does in walk. (It is only in trot that the head remains still, when the rider's hands must do so also.) In canter the rider's hands must move with the horse's head to allow him to move easily in that gait without hindrance and discomfort.

■ Bending exercises help you improve both balance and confidence

■ Perching forward and gripping
up

In the case of (b), the rider must keep his legs close
to the horse's sides to keep the pace going. Think of
your legs as accelerator pedals – if you took your foot
off the gas pedal whilst driving a car, what would happen? The car would slow down, of course. It's just the
same with your legs on a horse's sides – if you take them
away, your horse will naturally slow down, thinking
that's what you want.

With a lazy horse that takes no notice of your legs,
smarten your aids up with a tap from your schooling
whip so that he respects your legs.

Perching: 'Perching' means that the rider is hunching
forwards in the saddle, and sitting on his fork rather
than squarely on his seat; the position is such that gripping upwards with the legs is inevitable. This position is

one of self-preservation, and is often adopted when an inexperienced rider feels insecure – but it rarely works effectively!

Perching might be a reflex action but it is an unsafe one, as all your weight will be up and forwards of both your own and your horse's centre of gravity – therefore you are likely to feel even more unsafe and out of control, and are liable to fall off if the horse should slow up or swerve suddenly. Being aware of this should quickly promote self-control and discipline so you stop yourself from perching! To do so, instead of immediately hunching up when you feel uncertain or unsafe, take a couple of deep breaths to calm and relax yourself; then make yourself sit tall, keep your legs down and long,

and 'ride through' the difficult moment in canter.

When you have got used to doing this a few times you will realise that it isn't as hard as you imagined and feels much safer. Remaining tall in canter also means that you can direct the horse and control him far more effectively.

Beneficial exercises to do on the horse that will help you overcome perching are:

■ Have lunge lessons. Not having to control the horse will enable you to concentrate on your position without worrying that he will gallop off. Your instructor will be able to direct how you sit, so that you know what it feels like when you are sitting correctly.

■ Bending exercises in the saddle and on the ground will improve your balance as well as tone and supple you; you will then be better able to adjust your position without difficulty or fear of falling off.

It is important to use specific exercises in order to strengthen the abdominal and lower back muscles, so as to be able to maintain a tall position in the saddle. Without effective muscles in these areas you will have nothing in your middle to 'prop' you up. To illustrate this point, compare a tall, well established tree and a heavy flower bloom on a slender stem on a windy day: the tree will withstand the breeze and its trunk will

Leaning back: This is the opposite of perching. When you are initially taught to canter, you may be encouraged to lean back so you get the feel of how your hips should 'roll'. This is easier when you incline backwards, but once you can feel how to move with the horse, you should then bring yourself upright again. However, if you have trouble in remaining comfortable when sitting tall, or if you tend to be a lazy rider who slouches and collapses his diaphragm (rib cage), leaning back can become a habit. You may not realise you are behind the vertical, but its effect will be to send your legs forwards and off the horse's sides; when this happens, security, balance and impulsion will all be lost. Next you

■ *Left:* Bending forwards and backwards strengthens abdominal and lower back muscles. Both these sets of muscles help keep you tall in the saddle

■ *Right:* Leaning back: its effect is to send your legs forwards so security, balance and impulsion are lost

hardly move, whilst the flower will be blown about because its middle is too frail to control its actions – if the wind is the horse, and the tree and the flower are riders, you can see that the tree is better able to withstand the horse's movements and control its own, whilst the flower is too weak to do either.

Note: Ensure that you maintain correct posture in everyday life, whether you are sitting or walking. Soon it will become habit both on and off a horse. Not only will it feel better, you will also look better!

will find yourself becoming behind the movement and unable to control the horse effectively.

Overcoming this problem takes self-discipline and control (as does perching). Again, a person on the ground is extremely helpful and necessary to tell you when you are leaning back. An easy way to tell if you are sitting correctly is to look down at your feet – you should just be able to see your toe in front of your knee. Check both sides to make sure you are not sitting twisted and that one foot isn't in front of, or behind the other.

Problems of Position

The best way of distinguishing if you have any particular fault is to study photos, or preferably videos of yourself riding. Once you have determined which fault you have (and you are bound to have at least one!) you can then set to work positively to put it right, and then to promote the best possible and effective position you can manage, both for yourself and your horse's sake.

Looking Down

This is one of those annoying habits that often a rider doesn't realise he is guilty of – until other problems caused by it come to light. Looking down includes looking at the horse whilst riding it; looking at the ground in front of the horse; and looking through the horse's ears.

This last statement may surprise those people who were taught that the correct way to direct their vision was through the horse's ears. However, you do in fact have to look *down* to look through the ears, and if you continue that line of vision further you will find that you are inspecting the ground in front of the horse rather closely!

Looking down allows a whole host of other positional faults to develop, all of which have a detrimental effect on your riding and your horse. These follow-on faults are:

Carrying your hands too low: As you look down, your shoulders will drop forwards, therefore your arms and hands will automatically drop also. When this happens your hands become fixed and less able to move freely, and your contact with the horse's mouth will then become less yielding and effective.

Without a constant, efficient contact you cannot help the horse maintain an even rhythm, nor direct your horse accurately, nor ask for transitions and changes of pace successfully.

Slouching and gripping up: Slouching means that your diaphragm collapses, therefore immobilising your hip and pelvic areas. When this happens you cannot use your balance and position effectively so you start to grip upwards with your legs to try and compensate for your loss of security.

In gripping up, you then lose the effective use of your legs; it is an altogether restrictive position which has an

all-round effect on your horse, simply because you have very little control over what he does. Your weight is unyielding so you cannot use it to give seat aids; you cannot move with the horse nor feel what is happening under you; and you cannot give leg aids because your legs are not in a position to do so.

Because you are not in control, your horse can do more or less what he likes without you being able to do anything to stop him. You will be unable to direct him accurately, nor dictate pace and rhythm. Because all your weight will be forwards and over your horse's

centre of balance, he will pushed on to his forehand.

This means that he will be 'front heavy' and therefore unable to maintain impulsion, and he will be liable to trip up. If he does trip, you will probably fall forwards onto his neck, or will actually fall off, because you are not in any position to save yourself. On top of all this, a slouching position looks absolutely dreadful!

Negative thinking: When you look down you negate all forward thinking and planning as you cannot see where you are going, therefore you cannot prepare your horse efficiently and effectively. Looking down is a form of tunnel vision, where you set your sights on one area only and are, to a great extent, unaware of what is happening elsewhere around you. Therefore looking down, instead of ahead, is being negative – although many riders might not realise it. The phrase 'To look forward, not back' may help you to understand why looking down is a negative thing to do.

Your horse will sense your negative attitude and be less likely to respond attentively to the aids. He will also become worried, therefore tense, and this can show in several ways: he may become agitated and skittish; he may become withdrawn and sullen; or he may become nappy.

The remedy to looking down: A great deal of self-discipline! However, knowing that looking down causes all the above faults should give you the determination to cure yourself of the habit.

A remedy that one rider found worked for her was to remind herself to look ahead every few minutes. It took time and a lot of perseverance to make looking ahead, instead of down, a habit, but eventually she found she could do it almost without thinking, and with only a self-reminder every so often. And when she looked where she was going, it solved all the other lead-on problems she was also experiencing.

Wearing a correctly fitting stock can help you keep your chin up and your eyes on the way ahead, simply because it is too uncomfortable to look down!

Make looking ahead a real goal to aim for – but remember that you will not cure the problem without great determination on your part.

■ Looking down causes many problems, and is a habit that must be broken in order to make progress

Riding Out of Balance

Riding out of balance means that whatever pace you are in, you are not moving with your horse, or helping him balance, or feeling terribly secure yourself. Lead-on faults include looking down, gripping up and hunching up – all done because you are feeling unsafe. Being unbalanced also means you are not in control, therefore the horse is at liberty to do as he pleases, where and when he likes.

The horse will also not find it easy or comfortable to carry himself properly if his rider's weight is unstable and shifting about on top of him. At worst, this will result in him being more liable to trip, or lose his footing and fall; or he will be at real risk from strains, sprains and other physical ailments. At the least he will be unbalanced, and therefore likely to feel uncomfortable in all paces; unresponsive to your directions, as they will not be clear; or he may develop uneven paces and rhythm, and even become nappy as he learns that he can avoid working hard by unbalancing and unnerving you further.

Remedy:
The best way to cure this problem is to have some basic lunge lessons. These help a rider regain and perfect his/her balance and 'feel' at all paces, without the added worry of controlling the horse. Once equilibrium is regained, all the lead-on faults should also be eliminated.

However, once a balance problem has been successfully overcome, do not become complacent. To remain in harmony with any horse you must continue to work at keeping your technique up to scratch. This is to ensure that other faults do not creep in unnoticed – until you start to have problems again.

■ Riding out of balance means that your horse is not under control so he can take you where he pleases! Your horse is also at risk from strains due to your unstable position

Motorbiking

'Motorbiking' is the term used to describe a rider who leans inwards, especially round corners. Whereas this might help the handling of a Harley Davidson or a sea-going yacht, leaning in does nothing to help a horse's balance – except in an extreme circumstance where you may have to help your horse stay on its feet.

But what about show jumpers and gymkhana riders, you might say, who appear to zip around tight corners and make seemingly impossible turns by leaning almost parallel with the ground? Why do they do what we are saying is wrong?

It's a pertinent question! The answer lies in the related speed of the action concerned. Bear in mind that speed-jumping horses and gymkhana ponies have been

■ Motorbiking: leaning in has many detrimental effects on the horse, one of which is undue strain on his skeletal and muscular structures

■ Remain upright around corners and allow your hips and shoulders to turn into them. This rider has dropped her inside shoulder, otherwise her position is fine

highly trained and their bodies precisely toned up specifically so they *can* perform split-second turns at great speed – these are the extreme circumstances mentioned previously. Some of the movements that speed jumpers and gymkhana ponies perform are such that the rider *must* lean in dramatically in order for the horse to make the turn *and* stay on its feet, and for the rider himself to remain in the saddle *and* in control. He still keeps his essential weight in the saddle over the horse's centre of gravity, but puts a little more on the outside seatbone to prevent the horse falling too much to the inside.

For the ordinary rider and horse who do not participate in these activities regularly, there is no need to lean in at all, and if you do so it will affect the way your horse moves. Carrying a heavier load on one side is bound to unbalance him, as well as encouraging the unequal development of muscle. You will aid the horse more by remaining directly over his centre of gravity.

The fault of unnecessary leaning in arises due to a number of circumstances:
■ A novice who is trying hard to co-ordinate his aids and position effectively tries to take a short cut. He imagines that by leaning in the direction of where he wants to go, the horse will automatically go that way.
■ A stiff rider who cannot turn his body and use his aids effectively will lean in, in an attempt to force the horse to turn where required.

■ A stiff or unschooled horse may encourage an inexperienced rider to lean inwards in his/her effort to make that horse flex and bend correctly. This doesn't serve to help either the horse or its rider. The horse will not become more supple, and the rider in turn will not learn to use his body properly; therefore he will be unable to develop effective muscle formation, so will not be able to correct the problem.

A rider leaning in has several effects on a horse:
■ The horse will be forced to adapt his body wrongly in an effort to carry the lop-sided load comfortably. When this happens he will not be able to execute exercises such as school movements accurately as correct flexion will be non-existent.
■ The horse which habitually falls in and goes round turns with his shoulder leading (going through his shoulder) will be difficult to correct. Also this way of going will worsen the rider's position further.
■ Carrying an unequal and unbalanced load around turns will put immense strain on the horse's body and give rise to muscular, tendon, ligament and skeletal problems. The horse will also be at risk of losing his footing.
■ Unequal weight over the horse's spine will provoke back problems. Your saddle tree may also become twisted.
■ Because your horse will be uncomfortable he will develop ways of avoiding your aids and directions.

Remedy:
■ Consider how much it will cost you to replace your damaged saddle – that should give you the incentive to remain tall and square!
■ Think 'feel': are you putting more strain on one side of your body than on the other? Does your horse feel as though he is trying to negotiate turns without bending around them? (This will seem as though you are sitting on an unyielding bar of wood.) In this case you are probably trying to help him make the turn by leaning in, so as to encourage him to bend as you are doing. If you can feel some or all of these things, then you are bound to be leaning in rather than sitting up tall and square.
Without a doubt, trying to refrain from leaning in is a habit that

is difficult to cure, as you will be going against your instinct. Moreover, it is easy to make the mistake of trying to stay rigidly upright in order to beat the habit, and doing this is just as bad because you may then begin to pull the horse around corners with your hands, whilst you twist your body awkwardly to the outside in an effort not to sway inwards.
The secret. of remaining square in the saddle is to allow your hips and shoulders to turn the corner – even if your horse doesn't 'bend' with you. Keep your body upright and square – that is, back tall but without being stiff – and your shoulders and hips parallel with each other. It will feel awkward at first, but soon your horse will be obliged to become more pliant due to the way you are channelling his

movement through your shoulders, hips and legs. Eventually, by doing this, you will tone his body enough so he *can* flex and bend correctly as required.
To try and help you put this position in perspective, think of the way a river flows: the water flow has to go where the banks direct it. Now visualise each side of your body as the banks of that river and the horse as the water: this should illustrate how your body should work to keep the horse on course.
When trying to overcome your problem of leaning in, it is essential that you keep the pace rhythmic and slow. If you allow your horse to speed up round corners you will find it more difficult to maintain the correct position needed for you both to negotiate the turn properly.

Collapsing Hips/Shoulders

Remember how your position in the saddle was likened to three blocks on top of each other (Chapter 1, page 17): any displacement in this stack would result in the whole lot coming down. Thus if you collapse major parts of your body it affects not only your whole position and its effectiveness, but also the way your horse goes because your position is unequally distributed. It will also put undue strain on other parts of your body, as well as block the effective flow of your aids.

Although *you* may be unaware that you are collapsing certain parts of your structure, it will be apparent to anyone watching you because your position will be lopsided. More important your horse will be affected because as the load carrier he will have to compensate in his bearing and actions himself.

If you think about it hard enough, you can tell if you are collapsing a hip or a shoulder, because your horse will lean that way and feel heavier on that side than the other. He may also start to 'fall in' and be unable to flex properly, as in 'Motorbiking' (see page 87).

Effect of collapsing hips or shoulders:
- You are unable to direct your horse's movements accurately.
- You place undue strain on your horse's body.
- Your horse will soon adapt his response to your position and unclear aids, to the detriment of both of you.
- You will eventually twist your saddle tree and displace the saddle stuffing by placing unequal weight upon it.

Remedy:
- Lunge lessons will help enormously. Only by being told when you are sitting correctly will you learn to feel the difference between a correct and an incorrect position.
- Practise carrying yourself correctly off the horse so that it becomes natural to adopt the same posture when you are mounted. Only by toning your muscles, ligaments and tendons properly can you expect them to hold you correctly at all times.
- Make the effort to keep your shoulders and hips level with their opposite partners; then aim to keep them in line with your horse's shoulders.

- Collapsing hips and shoulders places undue strain on both horse and rider. It leads to all sorts of problems – most of them relating to control of the horse!

Wandering Legs

Most riders can tell if their legs are prone to wandering. For one thing you can feel them wobbling about, and for another they are never in the right place at the right time to give leg aids correctly and promptly! Moreover your position feels less than secure and tidy.

Effect on the horse:

■ He may not respond to your leg aids because they are inconsistent and unclear.

■ Your horse will waver about and be uncertain of his direction and purpose, simply because your legs are not directing his movement flow or maintaining his impulsion effectively. Accordingly, both his flatwork and jumping abilities will be affected. Remember that your legs are the accelerator pedals – if they are not operative, your horse won't go!

Remedy:

■ Use the 'football', and other leg-strengthening exercises off the horse (see Chapter 3) to develop effective leg muscles. Once you have the leg suppleness and tone you will be able to control your leg position better.

■ Practise bending and leaning exercises on your horse whilst keeping your legs in the correct position. This will promote your leg muscle development and strength so that you are better able to keep them where they should be at all times.

■ Aim to keep your legs relaxed, therefore long and better able to close around your horse's sides, so that they are less inclined to jerk around as you move your upper body. Allow your hips and pelvic areas to soften so that you flow with the horse and absorb his movement. Softening in these areas will allow your legs to relax, and they will therefore be less prone to moving around unnecessarily.

■ *Below:* Wandering legs are never there to guide the horse and tell him what to do

■ *Bottom* Try bending exercises, whilst keeping your legs in the correct position, to help promote leg-muscle development and strength

Heavy Hands

To have 'good hands' is applauded as a desirable asset for a rider, but what does the term mean, and how do you know if you have them? Basically, having good hands means that you maintain a steady, light and elastic contact along the reins to the horse's mouth. To be able to do this, your hands must be independent of the rest of your body.

If you are said to be heavy-handed, it means that you lack feel with the horse's mouth. Instead of maintaining a sympathetic elastic tension you tend to pull and exert unyielding pressure; you cannot tell when you must 'give' and when you should 'take'.

It is important to understand that whilst feel on the reins should be constant, tension is used in different proportions to indicate direction, to control bend, and to help balance or straighten the horse as appropriate. For example when you are turning the horse, your inside hand 'takes', *ie* a constant feel is maintained, whilst the outside hand 'gives', *ie* relaxes tension slightly to allow the horse to flex in the required direction. He would not be able to flex adequately enough to turn if you maintained equal 'straight' pressure on both reins.

If you drive, think about how you would turn a car around a corner: one hand brings the steering wheel round in the direction you want to go, whilst the other hand relaxes its tension slightly and moves up to allow the wheel to turn. If both hands remained fixed, you wouldn't be able to turn the car. To a certain extent you can apply this way of thinking to the way your hands must work when you turn your horse, the difference being that one hand moves back slightly as the other moves forwards. At the same time your hips and shoulders turn to the inside slightly in line with the horse's shoulders so that you remain all square on his back.

Where restraining aids are concerned, such as in a downwards transition, the reins do not pull back but simply remain 'closed' and quiet whilst combined leg aids and bodyweight adjustment tell the horse to slow down or stop. In the case of a walk-to-halt transition, your hands should stop moving with the horse's head whilst your legs send him forwards into this created 'dead end'.

If correct hand-to-mouth communication breaks down, it creates such problems as:
■ Your horse resists your hands and begins to pull.
■ Your horse becomes 'hard mouthed'.
■ Your horse becomes upset and confused when contact is erratic.

■ Your horse either puts his head above the bit or behind it (overbending) to avoid suffering a poor contact on the reins and to escape heavy hands.

These problems are caused by popor hand positions such as:
■ Having your reins too long or too short.
■ Your hands being fixed and rigid.
■ Your upper arms and shoulders being too stiff to allow your hands to move independently and to absorb

movement without jerking.

■ Your position not being independent enough, so you rely on holding on to the horse's mouth to remain balanced.

■ Fingers open on the reins which allows them to slip from your grasp, giving an inconsistent contact.

■ Inward-turning wrists which create a harsh, unyielding nutcracker action on the horse's mouth.

■ Crossing your hands over the horse's neck gives clashing and therefore confusing aids.

Remedy:

■ First of all, endeavour to keep your hands in the correct position by ensuring that a straight line is maintained from the horse's mouth, along the reins, through your hands and up to your elbow.

■ Next, to ensure that you maintain a constant and sympathetic contact, imagine that you are holding a bird in each hand. Hold it too tight and you will kill it, too lightly and it will fly away.

■ To avoid twisting or dropping your hands, check they remain in the correct position by keeping your thumbnails level with each other and pointing towards your horse's ears. A short whip, held horizontal to the ground and carried between your thumbs and your first finger, is another useful ploy to check the levelness of your hands.

■ Keep your hands quiet by relaxing your shoulder and the whole of each arm. Pretend you are holding a glass of water in each hand and don't want to spill it, so concentrate on keeping your hands still.

The golden rules to observe are that in walk and canter your hands should follow the nodding action of your horse's head, whilst in trot, when the horse's head is relatively steady, your hands should remain still. Achieving the right feel of when to give and when to take does require a great deal of time and practice – but persevere and you'll get there.

■ Having a poor and heavy hand position makes for a real breakdown in communication

Stiffness

To move comfortably and be effective on a horse, it is essential that the rider is relaxed and supple. If you are stiff in all or any part of your body, this will block any aids or position movement you wish to make. Very often stiffness seems to be prevalent in the joints, in the shoulders, pelvic and hip areas, neck, elbows, wrists, knees or ankles.

Where shoulder and/or pelvic stiffness is present, the rider will find moving with the horse difficult and will tend to brace himself against that movement instead of flowing with and absorbing it.

If you suffer from neck stiffness, you will have problems all the way down your body as far as tension and turning are concerned.

Wrist, elbow, knee and ankle stiffness will make it difficult for you to use the appropriate limbs smoothly, efficiently and effectively, therefore your aids will be adversely affected.

Effect on the horse:
With a stiff, unyielding rider on his back, a horse will find it hard to carry himself comfortably. He will tense up in an effort to brace himself against the hard mass above him banging down on his back, and directing him in a jerky fashion. Because of this, the horse in turn becomes stiff and unyielding.

Think which load *you* would find easier to carry on your back: a sack of odd-shaped iron bars; or a sack full of sand. Of course, it would be the latter, as it would mould to your shape and absorb your movement. To a horse, a stiff rider feels like the sack of iron bars.

Remedy:
■ A great deal of positive thought about relaxing is required here; you must allow yourself to become softer in the saddle if this problem is to be overcome.

■ If your stiffness is caused through nerves, refer to Chapter 6.

■ If you are stiff due to lack of body suppleness, make the effort to exercise appropriately. You will find helpful exercise examples in Chapter 3.

■ With a stiff rider on board a horse will find it hard to carry himself comfortably and will become tense himself

Rounded Back

Sitting like a sack of potatoes can be attributed to either of two things: it is more comfortable to do so because of a back problem; or you are just plain lazy! In the case of the former you have an excuse, but in the latter you clearly do not.

The overall appearance of a rider who slouches is neither pretty nor effective. Slouching leads to a jutting chin, perching, gripping with your knees and looking down – the effects of all these faults are dealt with in 'Looking Down', as previously discussed (see page 84). Sitting in this position will have effect of your hips coming up and forwards, instead of being correctly positioned up and tilted back. Only in this position can your pubic bone lift up, therefore allowing your bottom to rest on your seatbones. Slumping forwards means that you effectively immobilise your whole body and therefore are in no position to control your horse as you would wish!

■ A rounded back; not a pretty sight. Not only that but knock-on problems include gripping up, looking down and perching

Effect on the horse:
■ He will be pushed forwards on to his forehand, so cannot use his hindquarters properly. Because all your weight, and therefore his, is forwards he will be liable to stumble and trip.
■ Your horse will be unable to carry out the tasks and movements you require of him easily – if at all.
■ As you are in a position that can be dislodged easily, your horse might devise ways of doing just that.

Remedy:
■ Look at a photo of yourself slouching along – that horrible sight alone should provide you with the incentive to smarten yourself up!
■ Keep reminding yourself to sit tall.

■ Wear a back support to encourage good posture.
■ Look where you are goint at all times, as this will help you maintain a tall back.
■ Make constant checks that you are keeping a slight hollow at the base of your back by putting one arm straight across your back.

Lack of Rhythm and Co-ordination

If you find it difficult to work limbs independently of each other, you have problems with co-ordination. And if you cannot seem to keep your horse's paces constant, your particular problem is a lack of rhythm. It takes time and practice to get the hang of both rhythm and co-ordination; though bear in mind that the more you worry about not getting either right, the longer it will take to gel. That's because you need to be relaxed to achieve feel.

Think back to when you first learned how to drive, or to ride a bike. Neither was easy at the time, and probably you often wondered if you'd ever manage it! Well, it will help you to know that learning how to achieve constant rhythm and how to co-ordinate your movements on a horse is just the same. Suddenly it will all click into place!

Try to stay relaxed about your 'problem' – remember that Rome wasn't built in a day! The more you get worked up and upset about your co-ordination hiccups, the worse they will become.

■ A lack of co-ordination!

■ *Right:* Tunnel vision: unaware of what's happening around her, this rider is putting herself and her horse at risk

■ *Below:* If you suffer from co-ordination problems it's a good idea to go back to basics on the lunge. Then you can sort your difficulties out without worrying about controlling the horse at the same time

Tunnel Vision

1 Riders who suffer from this affliction rarely realise that they have tunnel vision. It means simply that you are unaware of anything that goes on around you, apart from what you have fixed your gaze on – which could be your horse, the way directly ahead, or the ground in front of you. Its effects might be as follows:

■ When performing a dressage test or jumping a course of fences, the rider is not looking around him in order to plan his next move or track in advance. This can lead to all sorts of problems, such as going the wrong way, performing the wrong movement, or missing fences out completely.

■ When hacking out, the rider will be unaware of potential hazards or objects lurking in driveways and hedges that his horse may shy at. This being the case, he will not be ready to take action as needed, and so is putting himself and his horse at risk.

Remedy:
The rider must make sure a concerted effort to remain aware of all that is going on around him, so that he can both plan ahead and take precautionary measures if necessary.

2 A rider who has tunnel vision can also be described as being acutely single-minded. This means that he fixes his mind on doing something *his* way, without taking into account that he may need to deviate from the path he has chosen to achieve the desired result. He may also be reluctant to accept that his method of doing things may be wrong.

■ In never thinking that his method may be wrong, the rider may persist in pushing his horse to do something it is incapable of doing, thereby putting himself and his horse at risk. At the least he could be creating deep unhappiness and dissatisfaction in both himself and his horse; at the worst he could be risking physical damage to them both if he pushes himself and/or the horse beyond their limits.

Remedy:
The rider must learn patience and to broaden his horizons. Taking advice and learning different methods is not a sign of weakness or lack of knowledge, it is an indication that the rider is striving to improve himself and his horse in the best ways possible.

Gripping Up

The term 'gripping up' describes an incorrect leg position. Instead of hanging down long and relaxed against the horse's sides with the knees lying open and soft, the legs tense and contract upwards so that the knees grip in tightly to the saddle. The effect is to shorten the legs and produce tension, so the aids cannot be applied effectively, and as a result, the rider is made to feel insecure in the saddle.

A rider will grip up if he feels unsafe or unbalanced, thinking that squeezing on tightly will make him more secure. In fact gripping up only serves to make the rider's position even less stable because he will be pushing his weight up on top of the horse rather than allowing it to drop down, thus letting the force of gravity balance him.

Effect on the horse:
Without the security and direction that should be given by the rider's legs plus the resulting unstable weight on his back, the horse will be unsettled, and also free to take advantage of the rider's insecurity and lack of control.

Remedy:
The rider will benefit from working on the lunge without stirrups to make his seat deeper and more secure, and therefore increase his confidence. In a nervous rider's case, this type of work should be done carefully at his own pace so that his confidence is not over-taxed.

Certain exercises performed both when mounted and when on the ground will help tone, lengthen and strengthen the muscles needed to keep the legs long, relaxed and stable around the horse's sides.

■ Gripping up results in the loss of rhythm, impulsion and control. If you tend to grip up, riding without stirrups on the lunge will work wonders

5

RESOLVING JUMPING PROBLEMS

The majority of jumping problems are caused by the rider. Horses refusing, running out, knocking down poles – all very often happen because of rider error. Certainly, there are horses who show absolutely no inclination at all to lift themselves over a fence, but more often than not, it is the human half of the partnership which is creating the jumping difficulties. However, whether your ambition is to go home with a rosette from the local clear round class or to qualify for the Newcomers final at Wembley, the principles are the same: that the rider should make it easy for the horse to jump. Thus the rider must create enough impulsion and ensure that the horse is balanced, he must present him correctly at the fence and keep a conversation going with him through the aids so he is in no doubt what is expected of him; and then the rider should not interfere with the horse. Watch a jumping class at any local show and you will see that many riders do not achieve all this!

We could give many examples of poor riding, and often the rider blames the horse – but in so many cases, if the horse is ridden properly, it will jump. A great friend of one of the authors runs a training centre specialising in jumping. Many so-called 'problem' horses and ponies are brought to her, yet only a tiny proportion turn out to be actually 'difficult'. In the majority of cases, once the riders know how to prepare their horses, jumping presents no problem at all.

The Horse's Jumping Style

Before going on to how the rider helps (or hinders!) a horse, let's consider how the horse actually jumps.

The quality of the canter: Before the horse is even presented to a jump, his rider must ensure that he is working actively, that is with his hindquarters engaged so the hindlegs are coming through well. The propulsive force comes from the horse's hindquarters and legs, so if you let him wander along in a long, flat outline with his hocks trailing behind him, he will have no chance of negotiating a fence properly. Once the rider has him in a rounded shape, bouncing along with his hindlegs coming through and under his body so that he is balanced and listening to the aids, a fence can be approached.

Remember that when a horse jumps it simply lengthens and elevates its stride. If the strides prior to the jumps are active, efficient ones, then the horse's jump stride can be of a similar quality.

The approach: Unless you are taking a fence on an angle for a specific reason – for example, in a speed class – give your horse the best possible chance of a decent jump by approaching the fence straight. Cross-poles are handy as a first fence, as they draw horse and rider to the middle of the fence.

It is the rider's responsibility to see that the horse approaches with plenty of impulsion, in rhythm and in balance. Speed is not required: coming in too fast usually means a strung-out horse who cannot keep his hindlegs coming under him as much, and who is therefore less able to jump. On the approach, the horse will lower his head and lengthen his neck so that he can judge where to take off for the fence. A

■ This horse's canter is not as active as it could be – see how the outline is rather long and the hindlegs are not coming underneath him particularly well

■ Compare how the hindleg is coming through here to that in the first photograph. The rider needs to aim at a rounder, bouncy canter in preparation for jumping

rider's hands must be soft enough to allow for this, but without losing the contact.

A horse's vision is such that he cannot see things at close range unless he does lower his head. In fact as the last stride approaches, the horse cannot actually see the fence because it is out of his visual range.

Moment of take-off: Providing the horse is receiving clear signals to jump from his rider, he now shortens his neck and raises his head which in effect re-balances him. Then the forehand is lifted, his forelegs are folded and the 'hindquarter' engine provides the propulsive power as the horse springs into the air from his hocks.

In the air: Ideally a horse should 'round' or bascule in the air over a fence, with his head and neck stretched outwards and all four feet neatly tucked up. A horse or pony which is presented badly at a fence and going too fast, will often jump rather like a deer – that is, more of a sharp up-and-down movement, with hollow back and head and neck pointing upwards.

Landing: In preparation for landing the horse straightens his forelegs – have a look at a picture, and you will see that for an instant the whole weight of horse and rider is taken by one of the horse's forelegs.

To re-balance himself the horse momentarily raises his head, and the hindlegs follow through in preparation for the next stride – for this, the horse's back needs to be supple. An out-of-balance rider who is behind the movement can be a nasty burden for a horse, often resulting in the horse bringing his back legs down on a pole.

The getaway: This phase in jumping is often neglected, yet it is here that the approach to the next fence begins. Riders need to think about re-establishing balance, rhythm and impulsion as soon as the landing stride is made, or the rounded outline will be lost and problems may ensue. Watch horses being loose-schooled over fences and you will see how they balance themselves naturally and jump well. But once a rider is on board, things can change drastically!

The Rider's Jumping Position

As we noted earlier, horses are not actually designed to carry riders – and especially over fences. We domesticated the horse and changed his lifestyle in so many ways that it is only fair to adopt the position which most suits him if we wish to partner him over fences. Fortunately this jumping position is also the most efficient and comfortable for us! As the horse jumps, so his centre of gravity shifts forwards slightly; so if the rider's weight is to stay in line with the horse's centre of gravity, she has to shift her balance from being just behind the withers and move it forwards, too.

This is achieved more easily if the stirrups are shortened. How many holes difference between your flat and jumping lengths depends on the depth of seat you have achieved, but as a general rule, shorten your stirrups by at least two holes for jumping. The effect of this is to close the angles at the knee and hip joints, so making it easier for you to fold forwards and follow the movement of the horse. Fence heights and spreads will dictate to what degree the rider folds. Think of him/her being like a W on its side, the arms of the letter being made up as follows: shoulder to seat; seat to knee; knee to heel; and finally, heel to toe. To help you achieve a good jumping position, think of squashing the W as much as possible.

In the explanation of the horse jumping we mentioned the desirability of him rounding his back over the fence and having the freedom and suppleness in his back to land well, with the hindlegs coming underneath him. To help the horse here, the rider keeps her weight just out of the saddle as he jumps, letting the thighs, knees, lower legs and ankles provide her with support. As he lands, so her knees and ankles act as shock absorbers, too. It is also important that when the horse jumps, the rider follows the movement, so arms, elbows and wrists need to be supple.

Try to keep the back flat and look ahead. This will help you avoid tipping to one side and unbalancing the horse.

■ Practise the jumping position at walk, trot and canter before you tackle fences. Ensure that your lower legs do not slip back as you fold forwards; they need to stay on the girth so that you can apply your leg aids. It is worth spending some time practising the jumping position, as unless you can control your position on the ground, it is unlikely you will be able to maintain it during 'flight'

Being able to hold a correct jumping position at trot and canter serves a dual purpose: it demonstrates that you do have an independent seat, and helps you to strengthen and tone your legs

Riding the Phases of the Jump

Preparing the horse to jump: The rider needs to maintain an upright position so that she can use her legs and seat to produce a forward-going horse in a good outline.

The approach: Newcomers to jumping are often taught to approach a fence with a slightly forward position in anticipation of the horse taking off. More experienced riders should approach with a secure but light seat, maintaining an even rhythm, the legs close to the horse's sides, keeping a 'conversation' going with him so he knows you want him to keep going forwards.

Think of riding the horse forwards through a tunnel formed by the legs and hands – this also helps you to keep him straight throughout the approach.

Keep a consistent contact with your hands quiet but soft. It is particularly important to keep the contact consistent during the last three strides – this time 'belongs to the horse': if you alter the contact, for example, pull back or drop it, then you have broken your lines of communication with the horse and he will react, most likely by stopping.

Take off: As the horse lifts his forehand off the ground and propels himself upwards, you need to fold from the hips in order that your centre of gravity moves forwards with the horse's. Think of pushing the stomach and shoulders towards the horse's withers – this should help to keep the back flat. Imagine flattening yourself down instead of leaning forwards.

Remember to look ahead through the horse's ears – fix your eye on a point in the distance if necessary, but try not to look down. The head is a heavy part of the body, so tipping forwards and looking down will be felt as a strong alteration in balance to your horse.

Looking ahead also helps to keep the weight evenly balanced. Hopefully your lower legs will remain in place, with the heels relaxed and down.

Do not lift your seat too far out of the saddle or your legs will be straightened and pushed forwards. Your weight may also be placed too far back which will result in your getting left behind.

In the air: For the take-off and during suspension it is important that your arms and hands follow the movement of the horse's head and neck whilst still maintaining a light contact. The horse needs freedom, but he does not want to feel abandoned by his rider: remember that he is used to his rider having a light contact with his mouth, and if this suddenly disappears he may lose confidence and concentration.

Sometimes a horse or rider may make a mistake and it is vital that the rider 'slips the reins' – that is, opens the fingers so that the horse has the whole of the rein; for example, if the rider gets left behind he should let the horse have the reins to avoid catching him hard in the mouth. However, normal rein contact should be resumed as soon as possible.

Landing: As the horse prepares to land so the rider should return gently to the upright position. The timing of this needs to be practised, and care exercised here so that the rider does not bump back into the saddle, upsetting the horse's balance and possibly injuring him too.

Coming back down into the saddle too early or too heavily can result in the horse catching the back pole of a jump; it may also affect his balance and recovery on landing, and could leave him with a bad memory of jumping. After all, if something is uncomfortable, why should he do it again? A horse has a long memory, and a poor rider bouncing about on his back is a good way of putting an animal off jumping for a long time!

Rider Faults

Many riders are keen to progress, and see jumping as being 'proper riding', with work on the flat as a stage to be completed as quickly as possible in order that jumping can begin. As a result, people often start jumping before they have achieved a good, firm, independent seat and inevitably, problems arise. As an example, let me describe the experience of a client of ours who wanted to do her BHS Horse Knowledge and Riding Stage II examination. This involves jumping a small course of fences (about 2ft 9in). However, she was very nervous of jumping and watching her ride, it was obvious why. Her seat was very weak in trot, and she could not sit in the saddle when cantering but bounced around, using her hands to help balance herself and consequently giving the horse very confusing aids. Thus a great deal of work was needed on her flatwork before she was ready even to attempt jumping.

The fact that a rider is jumping before he is ready is often shown by the following sort of occurrence:

Extreme anxiety: In a learning environment, both adults and children could well feel pressurised into jumping; they may be unhappy or anxious about it but are wary of speaking out – though with luck, a sensitive instructor may pick this up at an early stage. As an example of this, one young rider we know has a pony at livery and is joining in jumping lessons because 'everyone on the yard does'; equally, her non-horsey parents are keen that she 'progresses'. However, she is obviously apprehensive, expressing her discomfort with this situation by becoming extremely anxious before and during her lesson. A plaintive plea of 'Can we start with something small?' is often heard but not always observed – and when things get too much for her she refuses to speak to anyone or do anything.

Naturally this is non-productive for both her and her instructor. Not all riders are brave; and if you are not and your instructor cannot recognise or appreciate this, then you would be well advised to change to someone who does! As long as you ride well enough, and have good instruction on a sensible horse, jumping should be enjoyable. It will be different and perhaps difficult, but it should not be so frightening as to shake your confidence.

■ *Complete loss of position:* Riders ought to be able to maintain a jumping position on the flat before attempting a fence. And if, after several attempts on a schoolmaster horse, the rider is still unable to keep a reasonable jumping position over a fence, then more work is needed on his/her balance and seat. One of the best solutions would be lunge lessons, which are extremely beneficial to riders of all ages and abilities. Initially, work on the lunge will deepen a rider's seat and improve his balance, then this can be built upon by work off the lunge for short periods without stirrups

Lack of Commitment

Commitment and determination when jumping are vital. If you are going to jump, presumably you want to do it well – and if you don't, then why are you bothering to jump at all? If it was *your* decision to have a lesson or enter a competition then it is only fair and sensible that you try your best – anyway for the duration of the lesson or round. And if you are not particularly determined to make a good job of your chosen sport – say, show jumping or cross-country – is it really worth the time, effort and money that you and your instructor, and perhaps other people, will put in to help you?

Being wishy-washy when jumping will inevitably mean refusals or silly mistakes, which probably does not do justice either to your ability or that of your horse. So when you tackle, for example, a show-jumping track, determine that you will ride every stride of the way around: you need 100 per cent commitment every time – 95 per cent may not be good enough to get you over that triple bar you don't particularly like! And riding across country with insufficient commitment is a good way to injure both yourself and your horse. Solid, fixed timber fences are not to be approached lightly: positive, sensible riding is needed, and if you cannot provide this, then do not attempt cross-country courses.

■ Approaching a fence in this manner is asking for a refusal. Commitment and positive riding are needed, whatever the height of the jump

Feeling Nervous and/or Fearful

People who are afraid or nervous of jumping tend to be so because of the following:

- Lack of familiarity
- A bad experience (*eg* a fall)
- Poor instruction (leading to a lack of confidence or a fall)

Newcomers to jumping are nearly always apprehensive, and even those who have been well prepared by good teaching will be slightly anxious. This is perfectly natural – yet human nature being what it is, we do not like to admit that something *does* bother us! However, given the right circumstances – good, sensitive instruction and a reliable schoolmaster horse – a beginner should soon realise that jumping is fun.

The way to overcome apprehension is to do so *much* jumping that it becomes second nature. Remember how uncomfortable and impossible rising trot seemed at first? Yet now, it's no problem! Jumping can be just the same – but you do need to spend time practising.

One of the best ways to jump lots of fences and to improve your seat, balance, feel, suppleness and co-ordination is by doing gridwork or gymnastic jumping. A 'grid' is basically a straight line of several fences which are jumped one after the other. The distances between can be altered, so you may jump a fence and have one stride before the next fence, or your horse could be bouncing through with no non-jumping stride between fences. A couple of trips down a grid on each rein and you could have jumped twenty-four fences! The beauty of grids is that the fences can be kept small to bolster confidence, then perhaps the last fence will be raised, then a middle fence – and before you know it you're jumping higher and wider than you have ever done before!

People who lack confidence, due either to a fall or poor instruction, will also benefit from gridwork. Initially a grid may be no more than poles on the ground, for the rider to work over in trot and canter; then a small cross-pole can be added (as shown) about 9 feet away from the last ground-pole.

Neckstraps ought to be provided as a security measure for the anxious rider. Try to avoid holding on to the mane as this can lead to another problem – that of fixed hands (see page 114).

The instructor plays an all-important part in the building or re-building of a rider's confidence: he/she needs to know the pupil sufficiently well so as to know when gentle pushing will help him/her achieve a certain goal, and when stronger words or a more authoritarian attitude is needed.

It is also vital that a nervous rider has complete faith in his/her mount. In the event of a bad fall from his/her own horse, an analysis of what went wrong and why will help. The problem may lie with the rider, but if the horse is a problem – too fit, too highly strung or downright naughty – then sound advice on the best way forwards should be sought from an experienced instructor before the owner attempts to regain her confidence on her own horse. It's not a bad idea to go back to a reputable riding school first of all and regain your confidence on a trusted schoolmaster.

For those who have suffered a fall, it is too easy to let everything get out of perspective. Not many people suffer horrendous falls at regular intervals but if you are going to jump, the law of averages insists that your chances of parting company are going to be greater than if you stick to hacks on quiet bridleways.

Falls are a risk – but you can lessen their impact, and also reduce the odds. Firstly, be as well prepared as possible. This means:

- Ensure that both you and your horse are up to the level of jumping you are attempting. There is no point in entering a BSJA affiliated Newcomers class if you cannot get round a local novice show-jumping course clear and easily. Don't be in a rush to jump higher and higher. If you can jump a small course well and in good style, then your time in bigger classes will come.

Prepare for your class – at the show is not the time to try jumping three foot for the first time! Successful riders spend a great deal of time schooling at home, and only when they and their horses are ready do they put their work to the test in public competition.

- Don't be in too much of a rush to progress. When you are perfectly happy and comfortable jumping at one particular height; when you can cope with unexpected problems without getting into a complete fluster; and when you have done your homework thoroughly on the next height class, then you can move on.
- Protect yourself by always wearing the correct riding clothes, especially hat/helmet, boots and body protector. There is no reason why you should reserve your body protector for cross-country only; falls can happen just as easily in the show-jumping arena, and the ground is just as hard! Make sure you can fit your show

jacket over your protector. Remember to *practise at home* in protective gear, too; for your horse, protect his legs with boots.

It is also possible to learn how to fall off! Many injuries are caused by people putting out hands and arms to save themselves, and the end result is generally more painful! Often you know in advance that you are about to fall, so you do have the opportunity of relaxing instead of fighting against it. This may sound difficult, but a relaxed body hitting the ground may receive lesser injuries than a tense one. That ought to be an incentive!

Train yourself to curl up and roll – just look at jockeys who do this instinctively when they part company from a racehorse at speed. You can practise by rolling off your settee or over oil drums, and some riding schools do teach their pupils how to do this.

Fear of the unknown is often worse than the actuality: knowing what to do in a particular situation helps reduce the fear.

Lack of Confidence in Personal Ability

Riders of all levels can experience a confidence crisis, and it does not necessarily involve being worried about getting on or riding a horse. Some riders are quite happy about riding *per se,* but for one reason or another develop hang-ups about particular aspects.

For instance, one lady is more than happy to jump 3ft 6in cross-country fences, yet she is less than enthusiastic about show jumps of the same height. This is not particularly logical, because of course if a mistake is made when show jumping at least the fences fall down! Nevertheless, she only needs one bad show-jumping round, for whatever reason, to suffer a loss of confidence. Mind you, because she prefers natural fences she does tend to practise the jumping she enjoys and neglect the more demanding show jumping. The result is that she is not so well prepared for the show ring anyway – and another round with maybe a stop or a couple of fences down, adds to her negative thoughts.

The mind is an extremely powerful tool and it works against us very easily. The rider who jumps the cross-country course is more than capable of jumping the coloured poles cleanly, too – the problem lies in the fact that she doesn't believe she can. Riders can lose confidence in their own ability within a very short time. In actual fact their ability is highly unlikely to have suddenly diminished *but* they have allowed their mind too much freedom and it has got things out of perspective. Negative thoughts abound . . . resulting in negative action . . . which only reaffirms the negative thoughts: 'There you are, I'm just no good at show jumping'. In fact what is needed is a great deal of positive thought, plus an outside evaluation of the rider's ability. (See Chapter 2 for more help.)

Lack of Confidence in the Horse's Ability

Riding is very much a partnership, with both horse and rider needing to trust and respect each other in order to achieve harmony. If a horse loses faith in its rider this could manifest itself in several ways: it might refuse to jump or otherwise misbehave, it may perform badly or not at all. Occasionally riders lose confidence in their horses. This is quite likely to occur at a riding school – riders seem to have their favourites, horses they get on with and enjoy riding, and dislike certain horses, perhaps because a horse is above their current level of ability.

However, if an owner-rider loses confidence in his/her horse the problem can be more serious; it's not so easy in this case to swap horses. First, he/she must realise *why* confidence has been lost. Maybe it can be attributed to one incident – for example, if the horse took off and fell over – or perhaps it has been a gradually increasing problem – for example, the horse has become increasingly difficult to get round a course of show jumps, so that he now stops more than he jumps.

As with anything involving confidence, it is important to have an unbiased view on what is happening and why. Book a lesson with an experienced instructor, do what you normally do, and let him/her comment on the results. It is still possible that the rider is the problem, though there may be a physical cause affecting the horse such as a sore back or the onset of a foot condition. Do seek veterinary attention if this is the case.

Once the problem has been identified a plan can be formulated to deal with it. Most cases of this type do require qualified instruction: jumping is so much easier when there is someone on the ground to encourage and cajole.

Ground-poles and small grids will help to rebuild a horse's confidence; a few days out hunting or drag-hunting will put the spice back into a sour horse. Perhaps a complete rest is needed, or maybe the horse needs more flatwork to increase his suppleness and obedience.

Whatever solution is necessary, avoid the temptation to rush remedies. Take your time, set yourself realistic goals and time limits, and confidence will return.

Freezing

When a rider freezes in front of a jump and no longer gives the horse any instructions, the horse may: stop, run out, or cat jump – and you cannot blame him for doing so, since all of a sudden he was left at sea by his rider. But why might a rider freeze?

Sometimes this happens even to fairly experienced riders as a result of nerves. However, novice riders are more likely to freeze due to fear, for example, if they feel they are being overfaced – they cannot possibly jump that fence now that it's a spread and much higher than they've ever jumped before. Thus the reasons why a rider is less than perfect when jumping may be linked: fear can lead to freezing; or dropping the contact; or getting behind the movement; and so on.

To overcome this problem requires the application of mind over matter – see Chapter 3. Make use of the visualisation techniques, and condition the body to react to certain words: for instance, 'legs' or 'kick' if freezing is your problem. Think of any problems as hiccups, not as failures; once you start branding yourself as a failure you start believing it.

Set yourself small targets, for example, 'I am going to jump this small cross-pole and keep my legs going all the way!' When you achieve this tell yourself you're pretty good. Don't let that nagging inner voice interrupt with thoughts like 'So what, it's only a small jump, I bet you can't do it over a bigger fence.'

Tell yourself that you can! Don't you *dare* let negative thoughts take over! Besides, setting targets gives a structure to your riding and your re-building process. If, for instance, your legs fail you over one fence, go back to whatever you were doing before you had a slight hiccup. Tiredness can sometimes mean that you stop using your legs before the end of the course. If that is the case, try to include some swimming or cycling in your weekly exercise to strengthen your legs.

■ As the rider froze at the last minute the horse did its best, despite being abandoned. The result is a fairly uncomfortable jump for the rider, who has tensed up

Getting in Front of the Movement

Some riders 'jump' the fence fractionally before their horse does: in effect they are standing in the stirrups before the horse has taken off. This may be because they are over-anxious to get over the obstacle; or are worried about being left behind; or are stiff in the knees and hips so cannot fold very well.

Working through small grids will help here, whatever the problem. Exercise on the lunge can also 'open up' the hips and improve suppleness.

If a rider is tipping too far forwards as he/she goes over the fence his/her back will hollow, he will be unable to keep his legs in the correct position and so will not be able to apply the aids correctly. In addition, he/she could come to grief when the horse lands.

■ Trying to jump the fence before the horse and getting way in front of the movement brings its own problems. The horse is unused to being ridden in this way and it's signalling its unease with its ears and tail

Being Left Behind

This fault also stems from a lack of balance, poor timing, and insufficient co-ordination. Once a rider is working confidently down a small grid, the reins can be taken away and the rider's balance improved by sending him down the grid with arms folded, or hands on hips, or arms out to the side. If you do these exercises at home, make the environment as safe as possible: use a neckstrap for security; never do them unless there is someone else present; and do not attempt them if your horse is headstrong, and likely to disappear into the sunset . . . !

Providing the conditions are favourable, an exercise which some instructors use to help improve a pupil's balance and feel, is to ask him/her to keep his eyes closed as he goes down a grid. Naturally the pupil should have been down the grid already several times: but if he can relax he will find it surprisingly easy to follow the movement of the horse.

■ Getting left behind. As you can see the rider's bottom is towards the saddle cantle – being in this position over a larger fence could result in the horse bringing a pole down with its hind legs as its balance would be disturbed

Lower Leg Swinging Back

If a rider tips forwards onto his knees instead of folding over a fence, then his lower leg will swing back and up. This is not very satisfactory as it means that the rider's base of support is almost non-existent. Further, more of the rider's weight is then placed on the horse's forehand which may affect its balance; as the horse lands, the rider, being already out of balance, could easily go 'out of the front door'. Even if he/she does stay 'in the plate', the legs will not be in the best position to apply the aids and assist the horse in his getaway from the fence.

If the leg movement backwards is only slight, then asking the rider to think of pushing the lower leg forwards as he goes over the fence generally ensures that it is positioned correctly.

For a more dramatic leg swing, a short-term solution is to tie the stirrups to the girth with pieces of elastic. However, the basic cause is that the rider has an insufficiently deep seat and is stiff in the hips, and this needs to be addressed via lunge lessons.

Fixed Hands

Whether they are working on the flat or over fences, some riders fix their hands – that is, their hands do not allow for the horse's movement. They may be fixed due to tension or stiffness in the elbows, arms and shoulders. This can cause real problems when jumping as the rider appears unable to let the horse have that all-important freedom of its head and neck. As a result he will therefore jump flat, which is uncomfortable for the rider as well as the horse. Some horses react to a rider's fixed hands by fighting against them, perhaps rushing at a fence, or not going forwards at all.

If the rider's hand problem is caused by stiffness, then exercises will be needed to loosen the shoulders and arms – arm circling, lifting the shoulders up towards the ears and then dropping them down again.

Working down a small grid on a reliable horse, keeping the stirrups but without holding the reins, will show a rider that he does *not* need to hang on by the reins. If the rider rests his hands halfway up the horse's neck he will be able to feel to what extent the horse needs to stretch its neck over fences, and should then realise how important it is to allow for this.

Exercises such as jumping with the arms out to the side or folded over the chest, or reaching forwards along the neck and then holding imaginary reins, will build a rider's confidence and balance so removing tension. An instructor can help if necessary by calling out 'follow', and by giving the rider feedback on whether he was too slow to follow and allow for the movement of the horse's head.

Tipping to One Side

Most of us have a weaker side to our bodies, and it is quite common to see riders inadvertently tipping to one particular side. However, once you know which is your 'rogue' side, you can work on keeping it in check.

Ensure that you are actually sitting centrally – a rider can be sitting slightly unlevel and it will feel level to him because he has always sat like that! Ask your instructor to take a critical look at you, as you ride away from her. Are you sitting with your weight evenly divided between your seatbones? Is the level of your heels the same? What about the level of your shoulders and your hips?

If you do sit centrally, do you maintain this position around a corner or a circle? Or do you let your weight shift or slip to the outside. As you are tipping or twisting to one side, so you are twisting your spine and making it more difficult for yourself to fold properly. You are also affecting the distribution of your weight on the horse's back – some horses may even jump crookedly as a result of their rider's persistent crookedness. None of this is exactly making it easy for the horse to jump!

Many riders have a tendency to drop one shoulder or hip which, when jumping, will affect how the horse takes off (or maybe he ducks out to the side), how he lands, whether he hits a pole, and what sort of getaway he makes from the fence. The obvious thing to do to correct this fault is to look ahead, through the horse's ears; but people often still revert to their 'natural' position. In this case give the rider more to think about: as an example, have someone standing at the end of the grid (out of harm's way, naturally) and ask him/her to smile, wave, or hold up a left arm as the rider comes down the grid. The rider must call out what is happening as it occurs, so therefore *has* to be looking straight ahead!

Your helper may change what he does for each complete trip down the grid, or he may switch halfway through so the rider is kept on her toes!

■ Tipping to one side over a fence or on landing also disturbs the horse's balance

Looking Down

'Where you look is where you end up' is a phrase often used by instructors to try and discourage their pupils from staring at the base of a jump. Just like the horse's head helps him to balance, so our head serves the same purpose. It is also a very heavy part of our body and so affects our balance considerably – which in turn will affect the horse's balance.

In addition, when a rider looks down, he/she rounds his/her back – which is the opposite to what we are trying to achieve with our jumping position.

Use the exercise outlined for tipping to one side to help you (see page 114) – and remember: there are no instructions or words of comfort written on the horse's neck, or on the ground, or on the bottom of the jump, so don't look for them!

▪ Try not to look down or that's where you'll land – on the floor! If you make a mistake when jumping a course resist the temptation to look back – concentrate instead on the fences left to jump

▪ One result of being too far forward of the movement is that a rider finds it difficult to quickly re-establish balance and position on landing, which means that the approach to the next fence is affected. Remember the get-away stride from one fence is part of the approach to the next

Collapsing on Landing

Some riders betray their utter relief of getting over a fence by collapsing in a heap in the saddle the second they land. If all you intend to do is jump one fence, you can live with this, but if you plan to ride a course then you need to get your act together quickly!

The getaway from one fence is the beginning of the approach to the next fence, so it is a vital stage. Whatever happened over the last fence is over – you cannot do anything to replace a fallen pole or improve your style, but you *can* affect the fences to come.

Sharpen up your mental attitude and ride each fence as if there is another to follow: think of getting back into the saddle quickly, with your legs on, and of riding the horse forwards, in balance and with rhythm and impulsion.

An instructor can soon tell you whether you are taking three strides or five to achieve this. Working through grids helps you to polish up your reactions. If it takes you four strides to recover properly after the last fence, come down the grid again and get into action by three strides this time. Another useful ploy is to come down a grid and then have to turn for a single fence: the necessity of negotiating a turn engages the brain and encourages you to get back in the saddle quickly and ride on for the next movement or fence.

Lack of fitness may contribute to your collapsing; work some aerobic exercise into your day – 20 minutes will make a considerable difference.

Being Shot Out of the Saddle

This may happen if your horse puts in an unexpectedly powerful jump, and it can be quite unnerving. When you first start riding a horse correctly to fences, with the horse's hindlegs coming through well, it is much easier for the horse to launch himself and the end result may be something that you are neither prepared for, nor used to! It feels as if you are being launched into orbit – and you may need to slip your reins to avoid catching the horse in the mouth. At the time there is little you can do except rely on your balance and hope! However, with practice, both you and your horse will settle into a comfortable jumping method which is pleasant for you both.

Toes Pointing Downwards

A rider who is not really ready for jumping may demonstrate this fault, as might someone who is particularly stiff or tense. Their whole jumping position is lost, and they are therefore unable to apply any aids effectively. Work on the lunge to improve seat and balance is needed before any jumping is resumed.

Gripping with the Knees and Thighs

Again, a common fault if the rider has an inadequate seat, poor balance or is generally anxious about jumping. Unfortunately the result of the gripping is that the rider comes up out of the saddle, which makes the actual jump feel far more uncomfortable anyway. To overcome this problem, spend time deepening the seat on the lunge, and then build confidence by tackling plenty of small fences.

Standing Up in the Stirrups

Anticipating a jump, being over-anxious to negotiate a fence, and stiffness in general may cause a rider to stand up in her stirrups for take-off, instead of folding forwards in harmony with the horse. Standing opens up the angles at the hip, knee and ankle, so the rider abandons the jumping position for a much less secure and effective one; she loses the shock-absorbing abilities in these joints, and if the horse does misbehave then she is not in a position to react particularly well.

If anxiety is causing the problem then the rider needs to go back a few steps, for example, to trotting poles and very small grids, so that he/she becomes more confident about jumping.

Working through grids, thinking of sitting and waiting for the fence to come to you, helps the rider who anticipates a fence. If she/he tends to throw herself forwards on the approach to a fence, then thinking of leaning back a little on the approach usually has the desired effect of keeping the upper body in an upright position until the moment of take-off.

For stiffness, general exercising to loosen and tone the body will help.

Catching the Horse in the Mouth

One of the cardinal sins of jumping is to catch the horse in the mouth. The poor animal has done his job and has been rewarded with pain – can you blame him if he says 'no' next time! Poor balance and co-ordination are generally the problem; and the rider must seriously ask himself if he is ready to be jumping! Occasionally it is a genuine mistake as he has been caught unawares by a particularly powerful jump and unfortunately has not been able to slip the reins. However, if a rider is persistently behind the movement and the horse suffers from the rider's inadequate riding, then going back to basics and improving his/her balance, seat and co-ordination has to be a priority.

Resting the Hands on the Neck

If a rider is basically insecure in his seat he may take to using the horse's neck as a prop, resting his hands on it over a fence. Naturally, this affects the ability to follow the horse's head and neck movement; while he may get

■ To help her balance on landing this rider is resting her hands on the horse's neck which means she cannot go with the horse's movement nor control the animal as well

■ Suddenly throwing the reins at the horse on the approach usually results in a refusal as the lines of communication between horse and rider have been abandoned

away with this over smaller obstacles, it will become a more serious problem as the fence height increases. Work on the lunge and gridwork will help to improve the rider's seat; he might then perform the exercise of jumping through a grid holding imaginary reins and 'following' the movement of the horse's head, by thinking of pushing arms and hands forwards. An instructor can be telling him how successfully or otherwise he is achieving this as he goes down the line of fences.

Dropping Contact

Some riders throw the reins at the horse in the last strides of the approach to a fence; the result may be a

help. In effect, the rider has failed the horse: not only has she left him without any instructions, she may also have affected his balance, interfered with his concentration and rhythm, and adversely affected his confidence.

Abandoning a horse before a jump, in effect saying 'over to you now', may result from anxiety or a rider's lack of confidence in her own ability. As the consequences for the horse can be serious and long-term – a jumper may be turned into a stopper in this way – the rider therefore needs to remove the cause of the problem as soon as possible. This may be achieved by going back several stages and re-building confidence over smaller fences until he/she is able to perform consistently and positively at all times.

poor jump, a refusal, or possibly even a bad jump resulting in a fall. Through the reins (and in conjunction with the other aids) the rider should be maintaining a consistent conversation with the horse, telling him where to go and at what speed. If this communication suddenly breaks down because the rider has dropped the contact, then the horse is left without guidance or

Tension and Stiffness

Many of the problems already discussed – standing in the stirrups, being unable to fold properly and gripping up – have their roots in stiffness. Make use of the exercises outlined throughout this book to loosen up your body and make the most of your riding.

Elbows as Wings

A problem which some riders have is to stick their elbows out sidewards over a fence whilst their hands and arms remain fixed. The rider mistakenly feels that she is giving with her hands and allowing the horse freedom of his head and neck, though unfortunately this is not so. Long-armed riders are particularly susceptible to this fault as they often do not need to 'allow' as much as short-armed people. The following exercise might be tried to correct it: work through a grid, without the reins but holding imaginary ones. As the horse jumps, keep the elbows tucked into the sides and push the arms forwards towards the horse's mouth. Ask an instructor to watch and provide feedback.

Raising the Hands at Take-off

Riders may mistakenly try to assist their horses at take-off by lifting their hands. As the horse's propulsive power is provided by his hindquarters, the rider's efforts are a waste of time as well as being unsightly to watch and a positive hindrance to the horse. By interfering in this way a rider restricts the horse's forehand and indeed may catch the horse in the mouth, too. Gridwork with the rider working with arms crossed, out to the side, on the hips and so on – in fact anywhere but hanging on to the reins – may help to break this habit.

Fiddling on Approach

Your horse should have been set up for his fence well before the last three strides, so interfering at this time will only have adverse effects. Yet riders can often be seen with hands going everywhere as they try to readjust a horse's stride or speed in those last three strides. In fact all they succeed in doing is upsetting the animal's impulsion, balance and rhythm. The horse's concentration will be disturbed, and indeed he may lose confidence because of the inevitable jumping mistakes which will ensue.

If you feel the need to fiddle on the approach then something is wrong in either your own training or your horse's up to this point. Remember that between you, the purpose when jumping is to make the horse's job easier – and if, for example, your horse is unable to canter in a good rhythm, then he needs more work on the flat before you jump.

Perhaps it is your irresistible urge to interfere which is upsetting your horse? You must break your habit, perhaps undertaking gridwork without reins.

Rider Frighteners

Without doubt there are some fences which are intended to scare the wits out of the rider, and this is where mental discipline really comes into its own! You have to allow logic and reason to rule the day, and not succumb to that awful feeling in the pit of your stomach because there is a huge ditch/big triple bar/trakehner or whatever type of fence sets your nerves on edge. It is often cross-country fences which cause the most concern – after all, solid, immovable timber can be pretty awe-inspiring. Here are a few tips to set your mind at rest:

■ Remember that horses generally respect solid fences and give them plenty of clearance. In fact well-built fences are much safer than flimsy ones.

■ When learning to ride cross-country, make sure you do so on a reliable schoolmaster and start with small fences. When you have met all kinds of fences – drops, ditches, zig-zags, banks, corners and so on – in miniature, it is much easier to approach larger versions with a positive, confident attitude.

■ Ditches are often rider-frighteners. *You* know the ditch is there but the horse doesn't always – and will have no reason to stop and stare at the bottom of it unless you do the same! A ditch towards you will have the effect of making the horse stand off, so try to abandon nightmare ideas of upending yourself in the bottom of the chasm. Determine to look ahead and keep the leg on, and before you know it you'll be over the fence safely.

■ Drop fences such as a log on the top of a downhill slope must be approached sensibly. Get your horse into a short bouncy stride so he can pop over the fence and drop down neatly. Avoid the temptation to tip too far forwards, but stay in the saddle and lean back to compensate for the drop (tailor the leaning back according to the drop) – be ready to slip your reins if necessary so the horse can balance himself and to avoid catching him in the mouth.

■ Steps: if you have the choice, jump *up* these before coming down them. You need to ride the horse forwards with plenty of impulsion, but not speed, in a strong steady canter. Keep your leg there to help the horse, maintain a contact and stay light in the saddle. When jumping down steps, approach quietly and slowly with just enough leg to encourage the horse to pop down – extravagant leaps are not required! As with drop fences, do not tip forwards; this will interfere with the horse's balance.

The Horse with Problems

We have seen that the majority of jumping problems are caused by the rider, but although bad riding is a major cause of jumping difficulties there are other factors which contribute. These include the horse being afraid, in pain or tired, having incorrect or insufficient training, or just being disobedient.

The horse may be afraid because:

■ Too much is being asked of him ie he is being over-faced for his stage of training or his level of ability;

■ The going is too slippery or hard – if he has already slipped or jarred himself he will naturally be reluctant to jump;

■ He has lost his nerve – maybe as the result of a nasty fall previously (never forget that horses have extremely long memories), or something unpleasant happening at a previous fence;

■ The jump may be flimsy and uninviting – for example, a horse not used to water jumps will be reluctant to jump in as he has no idea whether there is a safe bottom to the water (the horse's natural survival instincts take over here);

■ A horse may have lost confidence in his rider and so will be worried about jumping.

The horse may be in pain, for example:

■ He could be lame or developing a condition which is aggravated by concussion, eg navicular;

■ His back may be sore – especially if he has had to suffer an inconsiderable rider;

■ The bit which is being used, or indeed other tack, may be causing him discomfort or even pain: for example, a heavy-handed rider who constantly pulls at his mouth.

Tiredness of the horse may result from:

■ Too much being asked of the animal in view of his fitness level;

■ He may be suffering from a virus, or the onset of an illness without apparently exhibiting any symptoms, or without the owner/rider picking up on them.

The results of incorrect or insufficient training will be demonstrated as the horse will stop, run out, become nappy, jump flat: it is the trainer's/rider's fault here for not adequately preparing the horse.

In fact when it comes down to it, all these reasons why horses misbehave could be eliminated if riders were more observant, consistent, knowledgeable, considerate and sensitive. There are times when a horse does just wilfully disobey instructions, but when weighed against the problems that riders cause for horses, the instances of this are very small.

■ Misbehaviour often results from the horse not understanding what the rider wants, or from fright or pain. Here the horse does not know whether the water jump has a firm base, or how deep it is, hence the refusal to jump in.

In Summary

A rider's faults, whether they are on the flat or over fences, often relate to each other – indeed some faults may cause others. No-one is perfect, *but* we can all help ourselves and ultimately our horses. Recognising that you have a fault (and probably more than one!) is the first step. Next you have to do something about it – seek the help of an experienced instructor. Trying to correct a problem without the benefit of someone on the ground is like trying to round Cape Horn in a storm in a raft.

You need to ride effectively and consistently: regular instruction will help you towards these goals. This book can only suggest remedies but as we are all individuals, and so are our horses, there is nothing to replace a good, experienced, sensitive person providing 'on the spot' help and advice.

■ Faults in position can easily be picked up at trotting-pole stage and then worked on before the horse and rider commence jumping

Tips for Competition Success

■ Determine to ride every single stride of your show-jumping round/dressage test/cross-country ride.

■ Know what is required of you in advance – that is, know the rules for your particular competition.

■ Do not put yourself or the horse into a difficult situation – prepare thoroughly before entering a competition. If you don't and you have a disastrous round, you will damage your confidence and will have to start the long process of rebuilding faith in yourself.

■ Limit the damage – if you make a mistake do *not* let it affect how you ride the next fence or the next dressage movement.

■ Keep breathing, or you will lose concentration!

■ Avoid last-minute problems by having checklists of equipment needed for various competitions. Write yourself a detailed timetable and stick to it so you are not thrown into a panic by the sudden realisation that you have forgotten to allow time to collect your number, walk the course and so on.

■ Have a pre-determined warming-up routine so your horse is as well prepared as possible before he enters the ring or arena.

■ Make sure your turnout and that of your horse is as clean, tidy and professional as possible – this in itself will make you feel better.

■ If nerves get the better of you, keep yourself occupied at the compatition. For instance, go and watch other competitors and see what you can learn from them – imagine you are judging them – anything to keep your mind off the business taking hold of you and stirring up the butterflies.

■ Ride into the ring positively and set off for the first fence as if you mean business: in other words, attack it (not with whips and legs flailing but in a determined way).

■ Whenever you are jumping and you find yourself in trouble, the golden rule is to keep your legs on, keep a good contact and look ahead!

■ Being stiff and tense has resulted in the rider being shot out of the saddle. Note the horse's ears too: the mare is wondering just what is going on!

6
THE NERVOUS RIDER

Do you regard yourself as a nervous rider? Check this list of typical giveaway signs and see how you measure up!

- An irrational and total terror of having to do something you are not confident enough to face or attempt
- Your mind goes completely blank
- You may feel panicky and physically ill
- You may suffer a loss of co-ordination
- You may sweat through fright
- You go rigid and tense up
- You frequently suffer from an over-abundance of adrenalin causing palpitations and hyperventilation
- You dread your next hack or lesson

To a certain extent, riding nerves can be healthy as they make you think before you act, helping you become a responsible rider. Everyone has them, but it is only when they begin to intensify and hinder your progress and enjoyment of the sport that nerves become something to worry about, making it necessary to try and overcome them.

There is a world of difference between having 'butterflies', and experiencing real fright when faced with something new. And for a person who suffers from a lack of confidence, there is nothing worse than being treated with derision or with a distinct lack of sympathy by an instructor or by other riders. This attitide is stupid and ignorant. The fact is that many riders would not be riding and competing today if they had allowed themselves to be browbeaten into not seeking the right sort of instruction and thereby overcoming their fears.

Overcoming or coming to terms with your nervousness can be helped by the horse you rider and the instruction you receive.

Basis for Fears

The main cause of nervousness stems from the fear of falling off and hurting yourself. Perhaps this has been brought on by witnessing a nasty fall or experiencing one yourself. Jumping makes many people nervous as there is a higher risk of having an accident. The second major worry is that you may hurt the horse through your own inability to do something.

Other worries may include: feeling self-conscious and not wanting to make a fool of yourself; being pushed faster than you feel comfortable with; having outside pressures put on you, either by parents or an instructor, to ride and do well.

Another common fear is that although you are drawn to horses and want to ride, you feel unsafe being close to the animal in case it kicks, bites or stands on you.

Once you know what you are frightened of, the next hurdle to overcome is how to cure or cope ably with that fear so that you can gain maximum enjoyment from horses and riding.

How Nerves Affect Your Riding

Horses can smell fear in a scent released by humans when they experience fear or nervousness. The scent is caused by a large release of adrenalin in the body's nervous system which prepares that person for sudden 'flight' or strength as necessary. In the olden days grooms used to dab aromatic oils, mainly lavender, on their pulse points to disguise any smell of anxiety or fear and to soothe the horse. It is worth knowing that a modern-day equivalent of these old aromatic oils is available from Day, Son & Hewitt (based in the UK), in a form called PAX. This is an aromatic coaxing fluid which is dabbed over a rider's hands, wrists, forehead and neck to counteract nervousness and fractiousness in horses and to disguise any smell of fear in the rider. From feedback we have received, PAX certainly appears to work! You should be able to order it through your local tackshop. At the present time, however, it is unavailable in the United States.

Horses will also sense nervousness in a rider's touch, position, voice and respiration, and will either become frightened themselves (the natural flight instinct) or take advantage of a nervous and ineffective handler or rider by misbehaving. As the horse plays up, so the rider becomes even more nervous and the vicious circle which ensues can be very difficult to break.

Tension in the rider caused through nerves will affect his position, so he will be awkward and uncom-fortable for the horse to carry; also his aids will be unclear and ineffective. That is why it is so important to feel and remain relaxed in the saddle, even though at times this can seem impossible!

Your judgement will be impaired if you are feeling too nervous, and this can bring about accidents. For this reason it is essential that you never attempt something you feel uneasy about; wait until you *do* feel confident and are capable of doing the job, so that you don't risk either yourself or your horse.

A rider does not have to be generally nervous for the 'jitters' to get the better of him. Experienced, confident horsemen and women often have anxiety attacks or at times total mind blocks, usually when competing. Although they are perfectly competent at the task they are attempting, they find that suddenly they feel incapable of doing it. In these cases pressure is usually the reason for this sudden inability to complete the required task.

Case History

Nerves show themselves in all sorts of different ways. One experienced rider found she completely switched off, both in mind and body when attempting the show-jumping phase of one-day events, in spite of being able successfully to complete the dressage and cross-country phases. Her reaction once in the show-jumping ring was either to make matchwood out of the course, or to forget it completely! After she came out of the ring she could not remember anything about her round, and she could not fathom out why she should be so affected.

This sort of performance was completely out of character, as she had no problem whatsoever practising over a course of often much higher fences at her trainer's yard, or at show-jumping competitions held indoors – it was just at outdoor competitions that the trouble occurred. The strange thing was that her behaviour was not consistent. Sometimes she could go out and win a couple of classes, before switching off and making a complete hash of a third. The more this happened, the more frustrated and tense she became, thereby putting more pressure on herself and unintentionally creating a vicious circle that became seemingly impossible to break.

Finding the Root of the Problem

The more the rider thought about her problem, the more convinced she became that her ring-nerves were the result of her not liking jumping in the 'fish-bowl'

atmosphere at a show. Combining this with the fact that she didn't want to show jump at all but had to do it to event, the problem promised to be difficult to overcome as basically she had no desire to jump show jumps in competitions.

In her case, show jumping successfully was a disliked and resented means to an end: so that she could event, the main attraction to her being in riding over cross-country obstacles. The dressage didn't bother her at all, but she did feel it seemed like a waste of time to bother with show jumps when the real test of ability and courage lay in the cross-country phase.

Assessing the rider's mental attitude is the first step to take so that the problem can be overcome successfully. In this case the rider was of a strong character and tended not to do anything she didn't *like* doing – that was her personal choice, which up to then had worked successfully for her. Faced with having to do a job she would not have done of her own volition, her heart simply wasn't in it.

Effecting a Cure

The obvious solution to the rider's problem was to go out and show jump as often as possible to banish her ring-nerves; however, this made no difference. She did determine that whereas she felt nauseous and excited before the cross-country phase, she felt absolutely nothing before commencing the show jumping – and therein lay the real problem. So how could she encourage some real emotion to surface that would sharpen up her performance?

Not doing consistently well at show jumping, and knowing the reason *why,* was a source of immense irritation; but in trying hard to overcome her resentment at having to show jump in order to event, she was subconsciously suppressing natural nerves, too. Thus she had to come to terms, on a comfortable basis, with the fact that for once she would have to do something she didn't like and initially make herself enjoy it; only then would she overcome her negative attitude towards show jumping and learn to think of it as being as testing and enjoyable as cross-country jumping. Only when this was achieved would her show jumping come up to the same high standard as her dressage and cross-country performances.

Instruction

As you get older you tend to become more careful, simply because you realise what risks riding can bring. Youngsters don't think of the dangerous aspects so much, so you can be forgiven for feeling envious when you see them galloping about and sailing over what look like impossibly high jumps with gay abandon.

In becoming more responsible and careful, you also experience nerves in that you worry about what could go wrong, and the consequences. However, it is important to realise that with sensible care and good instruction, the likelihood of accidents is reduced dramatically.

As a nervous rider you need to derive security, confidence and faith in your abilities from your instructor. You also need to come to terms with your own limits and set yourself realistic goals. If you are striving to achieve the impossible you will soon lose any confidence you do have, and riding will become

- To help you overcome nerves it's essential you find an instructor you can relate to

- Sometimes an instructor almost has to 'bully' a pupil into doing something he or she would be too frightened of doing normally, but which he or she is perfectly capable of doing. That little push from the instructor can make all the difference!

miserable instead of enjoyable. The whole point of riding is to have fun and enjoy yourself, so do not let yourself be pushed into doing something you don't want to do. If you simply want to hack around the countryside, do so and make the most of it! Do not be persuaded into competing, or trying to turn yourself into a dressage star if you know you are not up to it, or that you and your horse would hate it.

To help you overcome your nerves and come to terms with your limitations it is essential to find a good instructor, one who specialises in teaching nervous riders. If you are learning to ride or returning to the saddle after a fright, a good instructor will start you off on the lunge or the lead rein; this is so that you don't have to worry about controlling the horse, thus leaving you free to concentrate on your own position. Achieving balance and co-ordination, and learning to stop, start and turn a horse is easier to master on the lunge or lead rein.

Under this sort of instruction, taken at your own pace, your confidence will undoubtedly increase significantly. If you are taught how to stay on and control a horse properly, the feelings of fright and insecurity will be minimal.

To be good at the job, an instructor has to be a bit of a psychologist to be able to teach people to their best advantage. A nervous person has to be coaxed along and shown what she can achieve, whilst a more confident rider has to be made to understand why she cannot run before she can walk!

Although those are the 'ground rules', each rider is vastly different; what works for one may not for another, so the instructor has to assess exactly how he/she is best handled and what methods might work best. Constructive teaching is tailored to each individual, which is why private lessons are far more beneficial than group ones, in the early stages at least.

An instructor often has to feel confident for clients, and almost bully them into doing something they are too nervous of attempting, even though they are physically capable of doing it. The reason for this is so that the client realises that he 'can' rather than he 'can't'. Once the task has been accomplished successfully, it breaks down that barrier of self-doubt and establishes enormous confidence in the rider.

To do this, an instructor really has to know the client well, otherwise more harm than good can be done if the latter isn't ready mentally as well as physically. And for your own peace of mind, progress and enjoyment, it is imperative that you, as pupil, feel completely safe in your instructor's hands: if you don't, then find one you *are* happy with.

Your Horse

Owners who find their horse too hot to handle would be well advised to sell it on to a more experienced person; then either to buy a calmer animal (better too slow than too fast!) or take lessons until they are more experienced and knowledgeable, and also confident enough to have their own horse again. Problems start when people try to run before they can walk, and decide that because they 'can ride' they are experienced enough to own a horse. Often their first mistake is in buying something flashy, as a status symbol; the second is not continuing with lessons once they have taken the plunge and bought a horse.

Another mistake is to think that just because the animal behaved impeccably when they tried it out for an hour prior to purchase, it will behave like that permanently for them when they get it home. They fail to realise that the animal is bound to be unsettled for quite some time when it has changed owner, home, routine and surroundings, and that it can take up to a year or more for a new partnership to gel.

No matter how well-schooled or mannered a horse, it will not stay that way if the rider/handler is neither knowledgeable nor experienced enough to treat, ride and school it correctly. That is why it is so important for first-time owners, especially, to continue with lessons so that problems don't have a chance to take root.

▪ The more time nervous riders spend handling horses, the more confident they will become, both on and off the horse

▪ Owners who find their horses too hot to handle may lose confidence, and would be well advised to change over to a quieter animal in addition to having lessons to brush up their technique

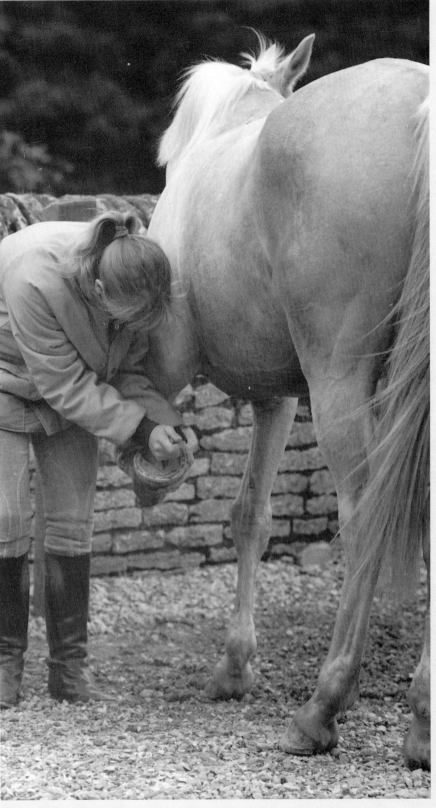

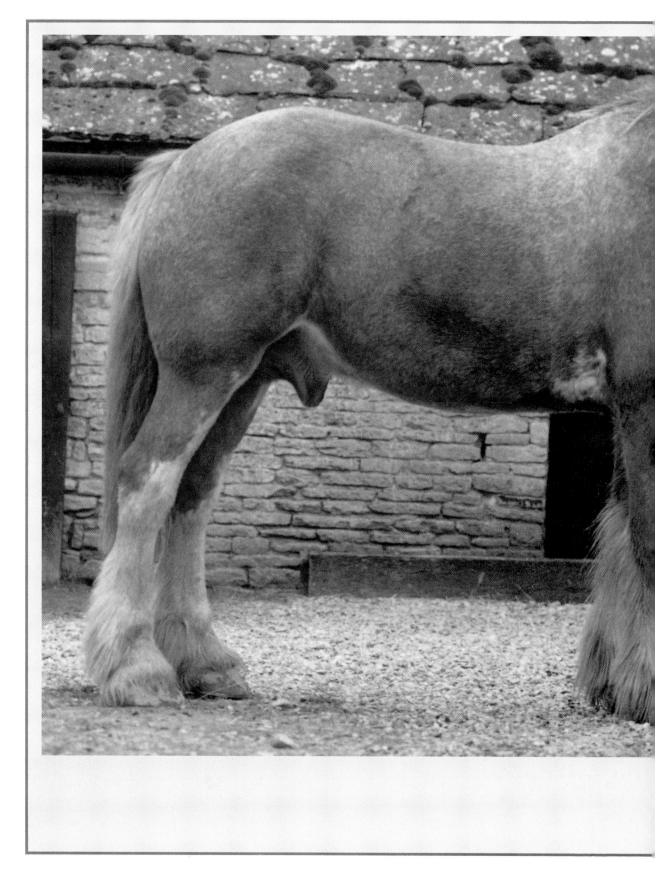

■ This type of kind, chunky and slightly 'dopey' (in the nicest possible way) horse is ideal for nervous riders

A nervous rider needs a schoolmaster horse or pony that is quiet, with a kind nature and well-mannered to ride and handle. Looks should be the last priority initially, unless he/she specifically wants something to show. Unfortunately trusted school-masters are thin on the ground, because basically they are worth their weight in gold; no-one wants to sell a 'good 'un' unless there is a very good reason!

The more time you spend handling horses, the more confident you will feel both with and on them. Avoid riding or handling animals you don't feel safe and at ease with – go by your instincts here. Treat your horse as your friend, and he'll treat you as his. A good sort of animal will look after you and forgive mistakes on your part, providing you always treat him fairly and kindly.

However, remember there is a definite line between being kind and being too lenient; for example, by allowing your horse to get away with pushing you around. If that starts to happen, you must nip it in the bud to prevent further problems occurring; otherwise you will end up losing confidence, and will own an ill-mannered horse.

Importance of Size and Type

Smaller horses are less intimidating than larger ones to nervous riders, so providing it is well up to your weight, ride a horse whose size you feel comfortable with. To find out how to tell if a horse is up to your weight, refer to Chapter 3 (page 51). A horse's paces should also be taken into consideration where a nervous rider is concerned: a quick and short-striding horse arouses the fear that it will bolt; the more laid-back and slow-striding the horse, the safer a nervous rider will feel.

As regards conformation, a finely built horse invariably fails to give the substantial and solid feeling of security that a more chunky animal offers, where the rider has more 'to get hold of'. And in temperament, the more laid-back the horse the better for a nervous rider. This sort of animal is less likely to jump about and shy quickly at things, behaviour which soon makes edgy riders even more nervous.

When you find a horse that you are comfortable with and like riding, half the battle is won!

Your Mental Approach

■ Set yourself realistic and attainable goals eg trotting poles today, a small fence tomorrow

■ *Opposite* Keeping your horse at a friendly yard will encourage you to mix with other owners and make new friends. This is the ideal way to boost your self-confidence and you will build a network of people you can turn to for advice and help

Knowing your own personal weakness can, with the right help and advice, make you a more positive rider because you can identify precisely which area you need to work on most – in this case your confidence. Any imperfections in your riding often turn into motivational forces as you strive to improve in other ways to help overcome your weakness. Riders who know what their shortcomings are, are the ones most likely to succeed in, and get the most out of, their chosen riding pursuit, whether it be competing or just pottering about for pure pleasure. Knowing your own limitations and how far you can push yourself makes you appreciate your horse's needs more. (Refer to pages 144–5 for additional advice.)

Many riders who suffer from nerves often feel 'useless'. However, it is important to realise that *no* rider is useless – it is only self-doubt and a lack of good instruction that causes you to think that you

might be! With suitable help it is amazing what you can achieve, if only to feel happier within yourself and proud of your achievements, no matter how slight.

At the other end of the scale is the rider who thinks he/she is perfect and has no need of help and advice. This is undoubtedly the worst problem to overcome, as that rider has first to acknowledge this flaw before he/she can improve – and that is the major obstacle!

Your mental approach is the first key needed to unlock the door to riding enjoyment and success at any level. The second is ensuring that you use only positive mental aspects to maximise your potential. Try hard to push any negative feelings you have firmly to one side and do not let them intrude. This will be easier to do if the combination is right, ie you have an instructor and horse you feel happy and safe with; also going at your *own* pace, and setting yourself *realistic* goals to aim for. Achieving these goals will give you confidence and restore faith in your own abilities.

Pick a riding school where the atmosphere is friendly and the attitude of the staff is helpful and understanding. And even if you have your own horse, make the effort to mix with other riders whose attitudes and ways of doing things are akin to your own. Keeping your horse at a friendly, busy yard, rather than at a quieter place, will boost your confidence enormously as you will probably find yourself obliged to muck in, whether you like it or not!

Tackling problems head-on, rather than shrinking away from them, is the only real way of building social confidence; withdrawing and hoping that they will magically disappear doesn't work – they get worse, not better, if you don't take steps to resolve them. Riding nerves are nothing to be ashamed of, unless you succumb to them and make no effort to make life better for yourself. If you ride at a riding school, tell your instructor about your worries and ask for help to overcome them. If this doesn't work, even though you try hard at lessons, then it is not *you* at fault, it is your instructor who is failing you. If this is the case go elsewhere.

If you have your own horse and your nerves are making life miserable either because your horse is misbehaving and you cannot prevent him from doing so, or you are missing out on fun because you don't have the confidence to take part in activities – get professional help. A problem shared is a problem halved!

Fear of Jumping

Very often a person is frightened of jumping because he/she has not been taught how to jump correctly from the start, both in terms of position and presenting a horse at a fence. Other causes stem from confidence-sapping or nasty falls that have left the person shaken or injured; being pushed to jump higher than he/she is capable of both physically and mentally; being mounted on a horse unsuitable for his capabilities. Also, a horse that regularly puts in a 'dirty' stop can soon destroy a rider's confidence.

One of the most important aspects of teaching someone to jump confidently is to ensure that the pupil progresses at his own pace and on a suitable mount. It is rare that anything is gained by rushing nervous pupils into doing what they already fear, so it is essential that for them, the correct groundwork is carefully and sympathetically prepared and followed.

A good, perceptive instructor can quickly assess the pupils in his care, and judge what is the best course of action to take with them, both to get the best from them and ensure that they enjoy the lessons, revelling in new-found confidence and ability.

■ A nasty fall or jumping experience is bound to shake your confidence. Restoring confidence is dependent on finding an instructor who specialises in teaching nervous riders

▪ Where jumping is concerned it is important for the rider to take things at his or her own pace so that confidence is gradually built up

▪ *Opposite:* Remember that you don't have to jump huge fences to enjoy yourself. Many events offer small novice classes or minimus jumping. The most important thing to bear in mind is to please yourself, not others!

▪ Working without reins or stirrups over a low grid will help develop a rider's balance and confidence

Back to Basics

It is important that the fearful rider is taken right back to basics and started on the flat, then over ground poles, on a well-mannered and quiet schoolmaster if confidence and technique are to be improved. Until the correct jumping position has been established comfortably in walk, trot and canter on the flat, then in walk and trot over ground poles, the rider should not be faced with actual jumps. This may take only a short time to do, depending on the level of the rider's expertise, or it can take months and months; but whichever the case, progress should not be hurried.

Working without stirrups and without reins (not at the same time) over ground poles helps the rider enormously in gaining balance (so that he learns not to jab the horse in the mouth) and therefore confidence, but he must be at the stage where he feels comfortable and at ease attempting it. Once he can work over poles without stirrups or reins, progression should be made to small cross-poles (which help the rider aim the horse at the centre of the jump) and then a low grid.

The rider should then feel sufficiently confident and in control to try tackling larger fences, and ultimately small, simple courses – adopting the same position and

approach to larger fences as to smaller ones, he can't go far wrong! The important thing is to maintain impulsion and rhythm. Confidence tends to increase each time a fence is jumped successfully – providing you are being taught properly, with the right equipment, and on a trustworthy horse.

Problems with Your Own Horse

If you are having confidence problems with your own horse – he rushes into fences or hots up at the sight of them, or alternatively if he is nervous of jumping – it is essential to enlist the help of an experienced instructor, either freelance or at a riding school. Without help you won't get anywhere – and that's a fact! Getting your confidence back and your technique sorted out on a schoolmaster, in an establishment that offers all the facilities you need, will help you enormously when you ride your own horse over jumps again. Then once you've got yourself sorted out, going for jumping lessons on your own horse is the best way of curing, or at least coping with, problems.

Setting Realistic Objectives

To set your mind at rest, let us assure you that you don't have to jump high fences to enjoy yourself or to take part in competitions and other horsey events, such as hunting or pleasure rides. Most of these events have small, novice-size jumps, and you can avoid jumping out hunting by going through gates or gaps in the hedge. If you don't feel happy jumping anything higher than 12in you should *not* feel embarrassed; the size of the fences you like to pop over doesn't concern anyone other than yourself, so you musn't feel inadequate or obliged to have a go at large jumps because others expect it!

Remember that jumping is only fun as long as you are happy doing it, are on a horse that you trust, and don't take unnecessary risks or over-face yourself.

Jump to please yourself, not others!

7
MAKING PROGRESS

Whatever their level, every rider experiences 'lows' as well as 'highs'. Sometimes the frustration can become so overwhelming that people seriously consider giving up riding. When it gets that bad, there is something very wrong with either the way the rider is being taught,or the way the rider who does not have lessons, for whatever reason, is doing things.

Riding should not be a stressful experience, but if it is you must consider why is you want to conquer the problem. Is it because you are trying to run before you can walk? Is it because you lack confidence and don't know how to improve it? Are you being pushed too fast, too quickly? Can you not cope with your horse? If you can identify the problem you are half-way to solving it, and this chapter will help you do just that.

Riding should be a pleasure, not a pain, but remember, you can only make progress and get good results if you go about things correctly.

What Are You Aiming for?

Where successful riding is concerned, progress is the name of the game. Upon reaching what you consider your ultimate goal, whether it is competing or enjoying a safe hack around country lanes, you cannot then afford to sit still and rest upon your laurels. Without constantly striving to improve your riding attitude, ability, techniques and knowledge you will find that you cannot maintain riding equilibrium. It is all too easy to become complacent about your ability and knowledge, then lazy; and before you know what has happened you find that bad habits have crept in unnoticed and are affecting the way you ride and the way your horse behaves.

On the other hand, trying to be too perfect in your riding is the source of great unhappiness and frustration – especially when you find you cannot achieve what you are aiming for. This wastes a great deal of time, because the time you spend bemoaning the fact you are not as successful as you would ideally like to be is time which could be spent enjoying the sport, and your horse if you own one, to the fullest. Trying to be successful at dressage when you would be better suited to, say, show jumping, or attempting to make your horse into a show-jumping star when he would prefer long distance riding, will cause a great deal of misery for both you and your horse.

If you do not have 'star potential' and/or the means to make it to the top in your chosen sphere, the minute you recognise that fact is the beginning of a whole new way of riding life. When you come to terms with yourself in the way of shape, ability potential and what you are happiest doing when riding, you then open new horizons for yourself. To go forwards, you must progress – not regress – and making notable improvement is dependent upon your being sure of your own limitations. Only knowing this can you use your mind logically to work out what is causing the hiccups. Then you can tackle problems head-on and immediately. Remember that a cool, clear mind repays in kind!

Every so often you will reach a plateau where nothing seems to go right and you cannot make any headway. Do not let this depress you – you may feel as though you have come up against a brick wall sometimes, but it is not an insurmountable problem. Time, professional help and instruction often work wonders, if only to boost your much-needed confidence; so don't be reluctant to enlist the aid of an instructor.

Making happy and therefore real progress can take many forms:

■ A rider who goes out and wins prizes yet is unhappy with her riding and therefore derives no pleasure from it is not making progress.

■ A rider who doesn't yet feature in a line-up but has thoroughly enjoyed her day competing on her horse and will look forward to attempting another show, hopefully improving her performance in the meantime, *is* progressing.

The difference is in being happy in what you are doing. If you are happy *and* successful, then great, but do not make the mistake of sacrificing real pleasure for, at best, empty glory. There is a great deal to be said for self-satisfaction in what you are doing – and not a lot of point in doing it otherwise!

Decide what *you* want to do and achieve in the horse world, and aim for that. If striving to reach your goal doesn't make you happy, think and re-plan again. You and your horse only live once, so you may as well make the most of it and enjoy life to the full. Remember, too, that although *you* have that choice, your horse doesn't, so *you* are responsible for *his* contentment and happiness too, and you won't enjoy yourself if he is un-happy. Life is too short for you to waste time being miserable!

■ Part of the enjoyment of riding is sharing the experience with friends

Gadgets

As far as progress is concerned, it may help you to realise that sometimes ability and natural aids alone cannot solve certain control problems. Let's admit it, there are times when it is almost impossible to persevere 'doing the right' things, if, for example, your horse persists in carting you into the next county with regular abandon! So, rather than feel a failure because you cannot curb your horse's exuberance when competing or simply hacking out, or if he is plain bad-mannered or naughty, it may benefit both you and him to resort to certain artificial aids.

These come in many forms, from the traditional whip, spur, different bit and martingales to training gadgets such as balancing reins. Used and fitted properly when needed, 'gadgets' have a time and a

■ Draw reins. Before using any gadgets make sure you know how to fit and use them properly.

place in enhancing the safety and enjoyment of your rides – for both you and your horse. Some artificial aids can be used for both riding out and schooling under saddle – for example, draw reins, certain trade-name balancing reins, the Market Harborough and the de Gogue. However, the Chambon can *only* be used for lungeing in, and the de Gogue is better left to the real experts.

Before using artificial aids, do take the sensible precaution of consulting an experienced instructor to ensure that you fit and use the aid correctly. Even different bits and martingales can produce adverse effects, rather than improve your horse's way of going, so you must choose any different items of tack carefully. But before you start to think about trying gadgets, ensure that your horse isn't running away from pain or taking advantage of your perhaps poor or unsuitable riding techniques. Having lessons regularly on your horse can work wonders and negate the need for gadgets.

When competing or hacking out a 'hot' horse you can increase your 'braking' power by using martingales and/or bit/noseband combinations that your horse is comfortable in and respects. When used correctly and thoughtfully, gadgetry will ensure peace of mind and safety of body! But if fitted and used incorrectly gadgets cause great pain and distress, so if you are unsure about using something, ask an instructor.

Timely Help

Occasionally it can take something out of the ordinary to put you back on the right track and restore faith in the sport and your own abilities. Something unexpected and perhaps accidental – such as suddenly coming across a method or technique – can put a whole new light on what you are doing; or perhaps you become determined to get to the bottom of whatever is going wrong and go out of your way to find a method of help to solve it.

How many times have riders been bashing their heads against brick walls to try and break through the obstacle barring the path of progress, then when someone suggests a different method, the walls have come tumbling down?

The following case histories illustrate these points and may help you gain real inspiration as well as urge you into 're-discovering' yourself and your horse.

Case Histories

Being bitterly aware of your riding faults and having difficulty in resolving them, or suffering recurrent discomfort or pain when you ride, can affect your riding mentally and physically. The following two riders, one a top instructor and famous for her 'Ride With Your Mind' teaching method, and the other a world-class three-day-event rider, both had good reason to give up horses for ever: Mary Wanless, BHSI, through disillusionment with her riding and teaching ability, combined with total exhaustion; and Virginia Elliot who could have lost her nerve, but didn't, following a horrific fall in which she broke her left arm in twenty-three places and almost had to have it amputated.

In Mary's case, a complete rest followed by a chance meeting with Dan Aharoni and Nuno Oliveira, trainers who revolutionised her way of thinking, riding and teaching, brought about her hugely successful return to the job that she realised she loved most in the world. In turn, Mary has completely re-vamped other riders' concepts of riding, and the relationships that can be achieved between them and their horses.

In Ginny's case, her sheer will-power and determination not to lose what she had worked so hard to achieve, plus the skill of her doctors, and her eventing friends who helped her to recover from her despondency, put her back on the road to success. It took many months, and also the arrival of Priceless and Nightcap, for this to happen, but Ginny won through in the end.

And what about Georgina Colthurst! This talented and remarkable young eventer suffered an almost fatal fall whilst schooling, remaining in a coma and gravely ill for two months, yet fought back determinedly and courageously to compete again some twelve months later. This story is even more amazing when you consider that eminent neurologists had given Georgina only a fifty-fifty chance of survival due to her appalling brain injuries. Even if she lived, they thought, she would most likely remain partially paralysed with the mental ability of a child.

These are stories out of the ordinary, and feature riders at the top of their chosen sphere; but the important thing is to realise that without positive drive, determination and perhaps a handy chunk of luck, these riders would not have progressed. To this end it is important for riders to remain philosophical where riding and horses are concerned, and keep in mind that 'every cloud has a silver lining' – eventually, and whatever the odds!

It isn't just top class and talented riders that you can identify with as far as problems go. Many 'ordinary' riders also have tales to tell about their own self re-discovery, tales that can give other riders new hope and inspiration. For example, Caroline Davis (co-author) had reached the stage where she felt that riding no longer gave her the satisfaction and enjoyment it once had. Riding was becoming increasingly painful due to a hip condition, whilst actually getting to ride on a regular basis was difficult due to work and family commitments. Her lack of fitness and loss of muscle tone was also a source of irritation and despondency. Then a chance encounter with a sports therapist, Jo Hodges, who specialises in developing both the human and equine athletes to their maximum potential whatever their 'disabilities', gave Caroline hope.

Following an assessment both on and off a horse, Jo was able to tell Caroline where her problems lay and what could be done to cure them successfully. To try and escape putting any weight on the affected hip, Caroline was slouching forwards, her chin and hips jutting out – but instead of easing any pain, this position was in fact contributing to it. Her posture when dismounted was not much better. In fact Caroline knew she didn't look right, but could not work out how to change things for the better. Trying to straighten up both on the ground and when mounted hurt, so she didn't bother. Gripping up with her thighs and lower legs, another bad habit, was due to stiffness in her hips and across her shoulders.

Jo got to work by palpating Caroline's body tissue and muscles to assess exactly where the problems lay. She suggested methods to improve Caroline's posture; to strengthen and protect 'weak' areas, and to develop correct riding muscle formation without pain or damage. Sticking to Jo's suggested 'body plan' was tough for a week or so until Caroline got the hang of moving correctly (points of the hip bones carried back and pubic bone up) and accustoming unfit and therefore shortened muscles to beneficial exercises. However, Caroline felt a huge difference, both on and off a horse.

Improving her look both on and off a horse and *without pain* permitted real progress that Caroline didn't think possible, and gave back something she thought she had lost: real pleasure from riding.

Many riders may not think of consulting a sports therapist to overcome any problems they might have. Certainly Caroline had not thought of it before, and had simply resigned herself to putting up with pain when riding, as other specialist but non-riding doctors had suggested. Perhaps you can learn from this experience.

Golden Rules

If you do become badly disillusioned with your riding, then slow down, take stock and think your way sensibly out of the confusion. Consider all the ways that may prove helpful in re-establishing your enthusiasm for what you are doing, then try them.

Do not school a horse if you are in a bad or 'down' mood: nothing will go right, at the very least you will feel worse, at the most you will end up taking your frustrations out on your horse, which is not a fair or rational thing to do!

Activities for the Non-Competitive

There are so many things that the non-competitive rider might do that he would be hard pushed to fit them all in. First of all it is essential to organise riding time into the daily routine. Routine in itself is satisfying, and you can take immense pride in how you turn yourself and your horse out, in caring for him and all his associated equipment. Just because you have no inclination to compete, it doesn't mean that your riding activities have to be confined to perhaps uninspiring hacking and mucking out!

The horse owner might consider any of the following:

Hire a cross-country course and 'play' with or without friends.

Join a breed society if this is relevant to your horse.

Take your horse on holiday.

Have regular lessons or get together with a friend and coach each other.

Get a horsey penfriend.

Join a riding club.

Try riding to music.

Set up your own non competitive riding club with like minded friends and acquaintances to hold activities such as spare saddlery/clothing sales, treasure and mock hunts.

Try long distance/pleasure rides.

Have a go at a new activity such as polocrosse, vaulting or Western riding.

Plan a baby-sitting schedule (if appropriate) with other horsey parents in your area so you can all have time to go out and enjoy your hobby in peace.

Enter photo shows.

Go for picnic rides with friends.

Find a reliable friend to hack out with, and give each other lessons.

Work towards horsey exams for self-satisfaction, confidence and the extra knowledge you will gain.

Non-horse owners can also enjoy a host of things to do:

Join a school riding club. If they haven't got one at your local riding school, suggest that they start one.

Organise a non-owners' riding club amongst friends – activities could include video evenings, quizzes, stable management theory, joint lessons.

Sponsor a horse or donkey at a rescue centre/sanctuary and follow its progress.

Go to major shows and events for a great family day out – you might pick up lots of tips at the same time.

Try your hand at being a show steward or fence judge at local shows and riding club events – simply ask the show secretary if they need any help. The always do!

See if you can help out at riding schools or livery yards to gain practical experience.

Reliable and patient helpers are *always* wanted at Riding for the Disabled groups – so try to give up a couple of hours each week to help out. Many disabled riders wouldn't be able to enjoy the sport if enough helpers were not available. Make the effort, and make their day!

Activities for the Competitive

Riding life and activities for the rider who likes competition can be extremely absorbing and interesting. Having lessons to further your competitive goals is enormously satisfying and helpful – and never think you are too good to be capable of learning more! Try activities other than your normal ones, to keep you and your horse fresh – see the lists above for ideas.

A Sport for All!

No matter what age you are or what ability you have, riding is truly a sport for all. There is so much fun to be had, whether hacking around the country lanes simply taking in the country air and enjoying the scenery on a steady schoolmaster, or striving to fulfil greater ambitions.

Remember, the sky is the limit as far as enjoyment and real satisfaction are concerned, whether you compete or not. You don't have to be a perfect rider to enjoy horses – they have so much to offer, and you have so much to offer them. Learn to be happy with yourself, and recognise that what you are doing is of benefit both to yourself and your horse.

Happy riding!

■ There are so many things you can do, even if you do not have your own horse. Riding for the Disabled groups always need patient, reliable helpers, and by giving up a couple of hours per week you will provide other with a great deal of pleasure.

INDEX

Page numbers in *italic* refer to illustrations

Acknowledgements

The authors' thanks for help given in the preparation of this book are due to:

- Angus Murray for his superb pictures.
- Grange Farm Equestrian Centre, Peterborough for the use of their facilities.
- All our models, especially Charlotte Dunlop, Kim Atkinson, Fiona Atey, Michelle Johnson and Jackie Holmes.